USDA

United States
Department of
Agriculture

Forest Service

Forest
Products
Laboratory

General
Technical
Report
FPL–GTR–151

Review of End Grain Nail Withdrawal Research

Douglas R. Rammer
Samuel L. Zelinka

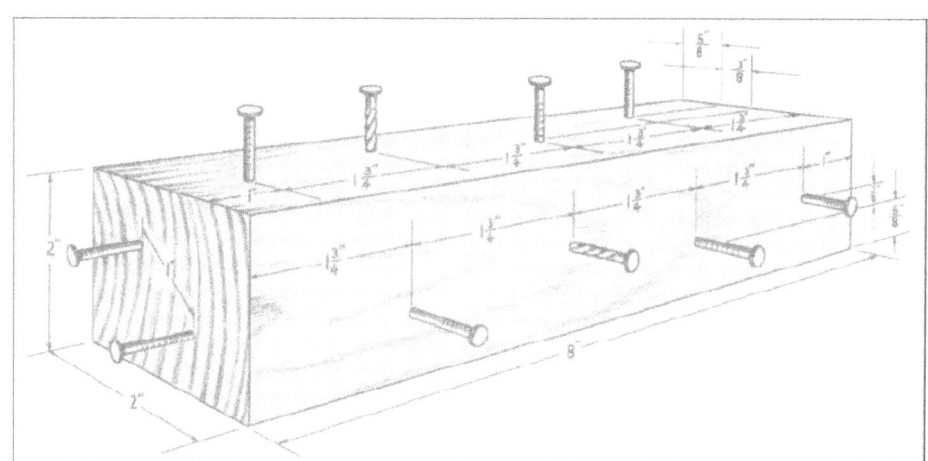

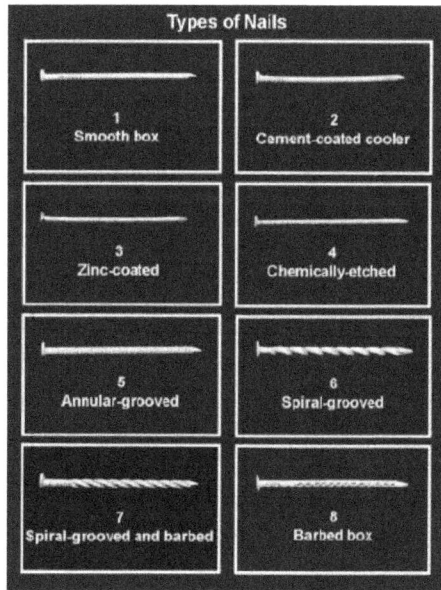

Abstract

This study reviewed the literature on static and impact withdrawal of nails driven into the end grain of wood members. From this, an empirical relationship was created relating the specific gravity of the wood, the diameter of the nail, and the depth of penetration of the nail to the static withdrawal capacity of nails driven into the wood and withdrawn immediately. Areas of additional research are identified for end-grain nailing in wood members.

Keywords: withdrawal, end grain, immediate withdrawal, nails, threaded nail, impact withdrawal, delayed withdrawal, moisture content, joints

Contents

October 2004

Rammer, Douglas R.; Zelinka, Samuel L. 2004. Review of end grain nail withdrawal research. Gen. Tech. Rep. FPL-GTR-151. Madison, WI: U.S. Department of Agriculture, Forest Service, Forest Products Laboratory. 28 p.

A limited number of free copies of this publication are available to the public from the Forest Products Laboratory, One Gifford Pinchot Drive, Madison, WI 53726–2398. This publication is also available online at www.fpl.fs.fed.us. Laboratory publications are sent to hundreds of libraries in the United States and elsewhere.

The Forest Products Laboratory is maintained in cooperation with the University of Wisconsin. The use of trade or firm names in this publication is for reader information and does not imply endorsement by the U.S. Department of Agriculture of any product or service.

Review of End-Grain Nail Withdrawal Research

Douglas R. Rammer, Research General Engineer
Samuel L. Zelinka, Engineering Technician
Forest Products Laboratory, Madison, Wisconsin

Introduction

Allowable design values for wood construction design specifications are based on a considerable amount of research. For the withdrawal of smooth shank nails from the side grain of wood, McLain (1997) summarized research since the 1920s and developed a new relationship between side-grain withdrawal capacity and the parameters of specific gravity, nail diameter, and penetration depth. McLain's research focused on side-grain withdrawal and did not speculate on how these parameters affect nail withdrawal capacity from the end grain of wood.

Currently, the National Design Specifications for Wood Construction (AF&PA 2001), which applies to the in-service performance of wood-based structures, states that the allowable end-grain nail withdrawal strength is zero. In certain applications, especially during construction, end-grain withdrawal strength is utilized to temporarily hold wood members together until the components are attached to the structural system. For these special applications, the designer or engineer must look elsewhere for information on end-grain withdrawal. One such source is the *Wood Handbook* (Forest Products Laboratory 1999).

Two statements in the *Wood Handbook* refer to nail withdrawal resistance from the end grain of wood. In reference to immediate end-grain nail withdrawal resistance, the *Handbook* states the following:

> When the nail is driven parallel to the wood fibers…withdrawal resistance drops to 75% or even 50% of the resistance obtained when the nail is driven perpendicular to the grain…

For delayed end-grain nail withdrawal strength:

> With most species the ratio between the end and side grain withdrawal loads of nails pulled after a time interval, or after moisture changes have occurred, is usually somewhat higher than that of nails pulled immediately after driving.

Though these statements about immediate and delayed end-grain nail withdrawal resistance first appeared in the 1935 and 1955 editions of the *Wood Handbook*, respectively, and persisted into the current edition, the underlying research and foundation for them has not been made clear.

This paper reviews past research on the withdrawal strength of nails from the end grain to clarify the statements in the *Wood Handbook*, highlights the knowledge of end-grain withdrawal strength available in both published and unpublished sources, and suggests possible research areas.

The first section of this report reviews research on the static and impact withdrawal of nails driven into the end grain of lumber and summarizes findings on lateral joints made with nails driven into the end grain. The following section addresses the effects of nail size, nail type, moisture cycling, time, specific gravity, and loading method on end-grain nail withdrawal strength.

Literature Review

The testing parameters, protocols, and results of all the studies listed in Table 1 are presented in chronological order.

Langlands (1933) reported the investigation of the relative efficiency of various types of surface-modified nails obtainable in Australia. Eight types of fasteners were obtained from six different manufacturers for tests in one wood species, western hemlock. Both impact and static tests were conducted at two time points: immediately after specimens were fabricated and 3 months later. During the 3-month period, the specimens were allowed to equilibrate to the laboratory environment. Eight types of nails were tested: plain, cement-coated, barbed, cement-coated and barbed, twisted spiral, cement-coated and twisted, rusted, and sand rumbled. The 12-gauge nails were 50.8 mm (2-in.) long, with diameters ranging from 2.62 mm (0.103 in.) to 2.77 mm (0.109 in.). Nails were hand-driven into the radial, tangential, and end grain of a 50.8- by 50.8- by 152.4-mm (2- by 2- by 6-in.) specimen. For each condition 20 replicates were tested.

For static tests, the nail was removed from the wood at a rate of 6.6 mm/min (0.26 in/min). For impact tests, the nail was driven through a 9.5-mm (3/8-in.) side member and removed using a pendulum impact tester. A constant weight pendulum was released that impacted and withdrew the nail. The impact energy for nail withdrawal was determined using the initial and final angles of the pendulum.

Table 1—Summary of pertinent end-grain withdrawal research

Author	Year	Nail type	Nail diam. (mm)	Wood species (no.)	Loading	Special conditions
Langlands	1933	Plain Cement coated Barbed Cement-coated, barbed Twisted Cement-coated, twisted Rusted Sand-rumbled	2.62	1	Static and impact	Immediate and delayed withdrawal
Gahagan and Scholten	1938	Common Cement-coated	2.49	57	Static	Limited tests with delayed withdrawal
Huston	1947	Common Cement-coated	2.49	2	Static	None
Scholten and Molander	1950	Common	3.76 4.11 4.88	1	Static	Wood joints
Borkenhagen and Heyer	1950	Box Cement-coated Chemically etched Zinc-coated Annularly threaded Helically threaded Helically threaded, barbed Barbed	2.49	2	Static and impact	Multiple wetting and drying cycles
Stern	1950	Common Annularly threaded Helically threaded	Various	1	Static	None
Stern	1970	Common Smooth box Cement-coated Uncoated Senco Plastic-coated Senco	Various	2	Static and impact	Delayed withdrawal
Whitney	1977	Plain	4.50	2	Static	Delayed withdrawal from joints
Lhuede	1985	Plain Coated Annularly threaded, coated Helically threaded	Various	6	Static	Immediate and delayed withdrawal

Tables 2 and 3 show average static and impact withdrawal loads, respectively, for nails in the immediate and delayed withdrawal tests reported by Langlands (1933). The tables also show the ratio of end- to side-grain withdrawal loads calculated for all nails and the ratio of immediate to delayed withdrawal strength for end and side grain. The side-grain withdrawal strength was considered the average of the tangential and radial withdrawal strengths.

Gahagan and Scholten (1938) conducted a comprehensive study on the factors that affect both the end-grain and side-grain holding power of nails. They evaluated the end- and side-grain withdrawal capacities of 57 wood species using both 7d common and 7d cement-coated nails. The average diameter of these nail types was 2.49 mm (0.098 in.). The nails were driven to a depth of 31.8 mm (1.25 in.) into the radial, tangential, and end-grain faces of the same specimens for determining immediate nail withdrawal strength.

The methodology used by Gahagan and Scholten resembled ASTM standard D 1761 (ASTM 2003), with the exception of the use of pilot holes. Pilot holes are not mentioned in the

Table 2—Static side- and end-grain withdrawal strength of various nail types in western hemlock (Langlands 1933)

Nail type	Nail diameter (mm)	Immediate withdrawal[a]		Delayed withdrawal[b]		Ratio of immediate to delayed strength	
		End-grain strength (N)	Ratio of end-to side-grain strength	End-grain strength (N)	Ratio of end-to side-grain strength	Side grain	End grain
Plain	2.62	489	0.50	271	0.56	0.50	0.55
	2.77	569	0.53	280	0.50	0.52	0.49
Cement-coated	2.62	547	0.53	249	0.55	0.44	0.46
	2.62	529	0.56	276	0.63	0.46	0.52
	2.64	542	0.54	249	0.55	0.45	0.46
	2.67	591	0.59	258	0.55	0.47	0.44
Barbed	2.62	436	0.59	289	0.58	0.67	0.66
	2.69	520	0.54	329	0.46	0.75	0.63
	2.77	542	0.58	298	0.59	0.54	0.55
Cement-coated, barbed	2.72	525	0.49	391	0.52	0.71	0.75
	2.74	520	0.53	307	0.55	0.57	0.59
Twisted	—	440	0.56	449	0.60	0.95	1.02
	—	547	0.65	493	0.66	0.90	0.90
	2.77	520	0.59	400	0.58	0.78	0.77
	2.77	498	0.57	413	0.53	0.89	0.83
Cement-coated, twisted	2.77	511	0.56	418	0.63	0.74	0.82
	2.77	556	0.60	467	0.60	0.83	0.84
	2.67	489	0.55	387	0.56	0.78	0.79
	2.67	480	0.51	427	0.58	0.78	0.89
Rusted	2.77	645	0.47	431	0.47	0.67	0.67
Sand-rumbled	2.62	596	0.57	271	0.53	0.49	0.46

[a]Nail driven into timber at 17% moisture content and tested immediately.
[b]Nail driven into timber at 17% moisture content and tested 3 months later at 13% moisture content.

Table 3—Impact side- and end-grain withdrawal strength of various nail types in western hemlock (Langlands 1933)

Nail type	Nail diameter (mm)	Immediate withdrawal[a]		Delayed withdrawal[b]		Ratio of immediate to delayed strength	
		End-grain strength (N-mm)	Ratio of end-to side-grain strength	End-grain strength (N-mm)	Ratio of end-to side-grain strength	Side	End
Plain	2.62	6,119	0.56	3,127	0.55	0.53	0.51
	2.77	7,079	0.56	3,692	0.57	0.51	0.52
Cement-coated	2.62	6,526	0.66	3,410	0.63	0.54	0.52
	2.62	6910	0.69	3,150	0.62	0.51	0.46
	2.64	6,774	0.63	3,173	0.63	0.47	0.47
	2.67	6,165	0.67	2,924	0.68	0.47	0.47
Barbed	2.62	6,560	0.62	5,092	0.73	0.67	0.78
	2.69	7,485	0.66	5,002	0.63	0.70	0.67
	2.77	7,181	0.62	4,629	0.68	0.60	0.64
Cement-coated, barbed	2.72	6,323	0.63	4,290	0.67	0.64	0.68
	2.74	6,063	0.64	4,042	0.72	0.59	0.67
Twisted	—	9,055	0.71	8,050	0.69	0.92	0.89
	2.77	7,215	0.67	5,442	0.74	0.68	0.75
Cement-coated, twisted	2.77	5,600	0.64	4,663	0.71	0.76	0.83
	2.67	5,724	0.68	5,137	0.73	0.83	0.90
Rusted	2.77	7,384	0.76	6,063	0.86	0.72	0.82
Sand-rumbled	2.62	6,594	0.59	3,579	0.58	0.56	0.54

[a] Nail driven into timber at 15% moisture content and tested immediately.
[b] Nail driven into timber at 18% moisture content and tested 3 months later at 12% moisture content.

Figure 1—Test apparatus of Gahagan and Scholten (1938).

description of methods, though their effectiveness is later evaluated. Therefore, the assumption is that pilot holes were not used in the reported tests. The report also states that the nails were driven by hand with "somewhat lighter blows than is common practice." Moreover, nails were driven directly into the test specimen, not through a faceplate. The withdrawal test was performed immediately after the nail was driven into the wood at a constant speed of 1.7 mm/min (0.068 in/min) (Fig. 1).

The specimens used by Gahagan and Scholten had been previously used in a specific gravity study utilizing paraffin coating. Therefore, instead of the 51- by 51- by 152.4-mm (2- by 2- by 6-in.) specimens specified in ASTM D 1761, the specimens were slightly undersized because the paraffin coating had been planed off. Moisture content ranged from 5% to 10% because the specimens had been oven dried for the specific gravity study. The report does not mention the procedures used to sort the specimens or any trend of splitting and checking in the wood from the drying process.

Tables 4 and 5 show average withdrawal loads for common and cement-coated nails pulled from three face orientations (radial, tangential, and end) for different wood species, along with specific gravity and number of replicates. The same set of 33 species was used for the tests on the common nails (Table 4) and cement-coated nails (Table 5). The tests on the

cement-coated nails included an additional 24 species for a total of 57 species.

Based on data from tests on 7d common wire nails, Gahagan and Scholten (1938) developed an empirical relationship that relates immediate maximum withdrawal load of nails driven into the side grain of seasoned wood or unseasoned wood that remains wet:

$$P = AG^{5/2}DL \qquad (1)$$

where

P is maximum load, N (lbf),
L depth of penetration of nail in member holding the nail point, mm (in.),
G specific gravity of wood based on oven-dry weight and volume at test moisture content,
D diameter of nail, mm (in.), and
A an empirical constant equal to 54.12 (7,850).

This expression, after applying a factor of safety, is currently the basis for the design withdrawal capacity for smooth nails in both the National Design Specifications (NDS) and the ASCE 16 Load and Resistance Factored Design for Engineered Wood Construction (ASCE 1996).

Gahagan and Scholten (1938) also investigated the effect of time between specimen fabrication and removal of the nail. In addition to tests to determine the immediate withdrawal strength of nails inserted into the side and end grain, they tested matched southern yellow pine and ponderosa pine specimens 40 and 105 days after nailing. As for the immediate withdrawal tests, 7d smooth-shank common nails were used for the delayed withdrawal tests. Nails were driven to a depth of 31.8 mm (1.25 in.) into specimens with 12% moisture content or green specimens. All specimens were stored in an unconditioned environment and allowed to air dry.

We assume that the fabrication and testing procedure utilized for the immediate withdrawal tests were used for the delayed withdrawal tests. Average withdrawal strengths of common nails pulled from the side and end grain after a time delay are summarized in Table 6, along with the number of replicates for each delay and the ratio of end- to side-grain withdrawal strength.

Huston (1947) did a limited study for the Army Service Forces, Detroit Ordinance District, on the holding power of common and cement-coated 7d nails with diamond points. The nails were driven into the radial, tangential, and end faces of southern yellow pine and eastern white pine specimens to a depth of 31.8 mm (1.25 in.). Nails were withdrawn at a constant rate of 1.7 mm/min (0.068 in./min), as in the Gahagan and Scholten study. Huston ran two sets of tests on the cement-coated nails. In one test, the nail was driven directly into the specimen.

Table 4—Side- and end-grain withdrawal load of 7d common nails in various wood species (Gahagan and Scholten 1938)

Wood species	Source (state)	Total number of tests	Specific gravity	Immediate withdrawal strength (N)				End/side strength ratio
				Radial	Tangential	Average	End grain	
Ash, white	AR	120	0.64	1,432	1,423	1,428	1,014	0.71
Aspen	WI	84	0.42	552	587	569	445	0.78
Aspen, bigtooth	WI	116	0.41	414	396	405	276	0.68
Basswood	PA	114	0.41	316	351	334	254	0.76
Beech	IN	120	0.67	1,134	1,068	1,101	770	0.70
Birch, paper	WI	84	0.60	1,179	1,090	1,134	832	0.73
Birch, paper	NH	60	0.60	1,108	1,121	1,114	636	0.57
Birch, yellow	WI	120	0.66	1,299	1,352	1,326	912	0.69
Cottonwood, black	WA	120	0.37	280	351	316	209	0.66
Douglas-fir	WA	144	0.54	552	614	583	347	0.60
Elm, American	PA	120	0.39	899	881	890	605	0.68
Fir, white	CA.	114	0.53	351	431	391	209	0.53
Gum, red	MO	114	0.39	770	770	770	556	0.72
Hemlock, eastern	WI	120	0.50	378	378	378	254	0.67
Hemlock, eastern	TN.	108	0.44	538	614	576	347	0.60
Hop hornbean	WI	24	0.76	1,637	1,601	1,619	1,094	0.68
Magnolia, sweet bay	FL	78	0.44	716	738	727	520	0.72
Maple, black	IN	18	0.62	1,419	1,472	1,446	1,041	0.72
Maple, silver	WI	120	0.51	667	823	745	605	0.81
Maple, sugar	IN	96	0.65	1,446	1,699	1,572	1,157	0.74
Oak, white	AR	96	0.70	1,161	1,179	1,170	818	0.70
Oak, white	LA	96	0.73	1,370	1,188	1,279	676	0.53
Pine, jack	WI	108	0.46	538	632	585	414	0.71
Pine, longleaf	LA	120	0.61	823	881	852	454	0.53
Pine, Norway	WI	120	0.51	512	596	554	391	0.71
Pine, ponderosa	CA	120	0.43	369	374	371	240	0.65
Pine, shortleaf	LA	78	0.58	774	956	865	534	0.62
Pine, slash	FL	96	0.68	783	916	850	454	0.53
Pine, southern white	WI	114	0.39	391	396	394	267	0.68
Popular, yellow	TN	120	0.42	480	507	494	347	0.70
Redwood (virgin)	CA	144	0.43	627	667	647	302	0.47
Redwood (virgin)	CA	240	0.41	787	730	758	391	0.52
Redwood (2nd growth)	CA	180	0.36	556	672	614	307	0.50
Redwood (2nd growth)	CA	300	0.32	427	534	480	294	0.61
Spruce, Engelmann	CO	120	0.36	409	405	407	325	0.80
Spruce, red	TN	114	0.41	436	463	449	276	0.61
Spruce, white	WI	108	0.43	529	552	540	391	0.72
Sycamore	TN	120	0.55	712	907	810	578	0.71

Table 5—Side- and end-grain withdrawal load of 7d cement-coated nails in various wood species (Gahagan and Scholten 1938)

Wood species	Specific gravity	Moisture content (%)	Replicates	Immediate withdrawal strength (N)				End/side strength ratio
				Radial	Tangential	Average	End grain	
Ash, white	0.64	8.9	114	2,024	2,011	2,019	1,713	0.85
Aspen	0.39	5.8	318	832	894	863	520	0.60
Aspen, bigtooth	0.41	6.5	120	899	921	907	698	0.77
Basswood	0.41	6.5	120	885	863	872	614	0.70
Beech	0.67	8.4	120	2,202	2,046	2,126	1,592	0.75
Birch, paper	0.60	6.3	138	1,975	2,002	1,988	1,299	0.65
Birch, yellow	0.66	7.4	324	2,082	2,002	2,042	1,428	0.70
Cedar, western red	0.34	7.6	228	854	899	876	525	0.60
Cedar, northern white	0.32	9.3	108	681	712	694	458	0.66
Chestnut	0.45	9.2	240	1,148	1,214	1,183	765	0.65
Cottonwood, black	0.37	5.9	120	863	872	867	543	0.63
Cottonwood, eastern	0.34	6.8	90	841	876	859	636	0.74
Cypress, southern	0.47	8.3	240	1,183	1,294	1,241	641	0.52
Douglas-fir	0.51	6.3	1,104	1,214	1,317	1,263	814	0.64
Elm, American	0.54	8.2	120	1,530	1,508	1,521	1,050	0.69
Fir, California red	0.37	9.0	90	787	841	814	445	0.55
Fir, noble	0.41	9.3	120	1,001	988	996	503	0.50
Fir, silver	0.40	4.9	90	894	921	907	383	0.42
Fir, white	0.38	8.0	198	783	903	841	463	0.55
Fir, lowland white	0.36	5.3	90	667	810	738	267	0.36
Gum, red	0.52	8.6	1,074	1,312	1,281	1,299	818	0.63
Gum, tupelo	0.52	7.5	288	1,619	1,495	1,557	1,023	0.66
Hemlock, eastern	0.42	8.7	1,542	1,005	1,036	1,023	565	0.55
Hemlock, western	0.46	5.9	576	1,210	1,246	1,228	676	0.55
Hop hornbean	0.76	6.5	24	2,282	2,135	2,206	2,033	0.92
Larch, western	0.58	4.4	90	1,330	1,419	1,375	801	0.58
Locust, black	0.71	4.1	72	2,051	1,535	1,793	1,797	1.00
Locust, honey	0.76	6.5	18	2,260	1,997	2,126	1,917	0.90
Magnolia, cucumber	0.52	5.1	120	1,557	1,490	1,521	1,036	0.68
Magnolia, evergreen	0.53	5.0	48	1,802	1,842	1,824	1,423	0.78
Magnolia, sweet bay	0.44	8.4	78	1,415	1,419	1,415	850	0.60
Maple, black	0.62	9.8	24	2,135	1,846	1,988	1,588	0.80
Maple, silver	0.51	6.8	120	1,481	1,503	1,495	1,246	0.83
Maple, sugar	0.65	9.2	96	2,211	2,042	2,126	1,761	0.83
Oak, red	0.66	8.4	438	2,073	1,877	1,975	1,388	0.70
Oak, white	0.72	8.6	192	2,206	1,975	2,091	1,423	0.68
Pine, jack	0.46	7.6	114	1,014	1,210	1,112	716	0.64
Pine, loblolly	0.59	7.7	824	1,214	1,463	1,339	663	0.50
Pine, lodgepole	0.44	6.3	180	1,085	1,121	1,103	627	0.57
Pine, longleaf	0.64	7.7	1,494	1,610	1,673	1,641	1,085	0.66
Pine, mountain	0.55	7.1	120	1,415	1,468	1,441	930	0.65
Pine, Norway	0.51	7.4	120	1,214	1,254	1,237	734	0.59
Pine, pitch	0.54	7.7	120	1,446	1,468	1,459	1,045	0.72
Pine, pond	0.57	7.5	120	1,548	1,713	1,628	939	0.58
Pine, ponderosa	0.42	7.5	600	1,032	1,045	1,036	605	0.58
Pine, shortleaf	0.58	7.2	144	1,472	1,650	1,561	1,045	0.67
Pine, slash	0.68	7.6	120	1,584	1,868	1,726	1,290	0.75
Pine, northern white	0.36	6.4	216	988	1,014	1,001	565	0.56
Pine, western white	0.45	8.2	120	1,134	1,094	1,112	596	0.54
Poplar, yellow	0.42	7.3	120	943	992	965	721	0.75
Redwood (virgin)	0.42	6.0	384	983	1,005	996	472	0.47
Redwood (2nd growth)	0.34	6.2	480	796	970	881	400	0.45
Spruce, Engelmann	0.36	9.4	120	787	818	801	605	0.76
Spruce, red	0.41	10.7	114	1,019	983	1,001	658	0.66
Spruce, Sitka	0.37	8.9	120	832	947	890	449	0.51
Spruce, white	0.43	7.6	114	930	970	947	649	0.69
Sycamore	0.55	7.0	120	1,641	1,552	1,597	1,201	0.75

Table 6—Withdrawal load of 7d common nails in ponderosa pine and southern yellow pine for two fabrication moisture conditions and three test intervals (Gahagan and Scholten 1938)

Wood species	Fabrication condition	Time between fabrication and tests	Total nails tested	Moisture content (%)	Side-grain strength (N)	End-grain strength (N)	End/side strength ratio
Ponderosa pine	Green	Immediate	160	30.7	578	338	0.58
		40 days	160	6.3	102	93	0.91
		105 days	160	5.5	111	178	1.60
	Dry	Immediate	180	7.8	440	289	0.66
		40 days	150	5.5	445	476	1.07
		105 days	150	5.3	743	632	0.85
Southern yellow pine	Green	Immediate	192	71.7	805	414	0.51
		40 days	160	9.2	205	151	0.74
		105 days	160	11.0	240	165	0.69
	Dry	Immediate	180	11.1	756	440	0.58
		40 days	150	11.8	712	431	0.61
		105 days	150	10.8	658	458	0.70

Table 7—Withdrawal load of 7d nails in eastern white pine and southern yellow pine (Huston 1947)

			Average withdrawal strength (N)		
				Cement-coated nails	
Wood species	Face orientation	Number of replicates	Plain nails	Driven directly into specimen	Driven through face board
Eastern white pine	Tangential	12	254	489	485
	Radial	12	209	503	507
	Side grain		231	496	496
	End grain	12	160	294	311
	End/side strength ratio		0.69	0.59	0.63
Southern yellow pine	Tangential	12	805	1,050	832
	Radial	12	730	916	761
	Side grain		767	983	796
	End grain	12	467	663	556
	End/side strength ratio		0.61	0.67	0.70

In the other test, the nail was driven through a face board to determine whether the coating would remain intact. After the nail was driven to a depth of 31.8 mm (1.25 in.), the face board was broken off.

Average withdrawal load values for the two types of nails pulled from three face orientations, along with the number of replicates for each nail type, are reported in Table 7. The table also provides the ratio of end- to side-grain withdrawal load. Here and elsewhere, side-grain withdrawal load is the average of tangential and radial withdrawal load values.

Borkenhagen and Heyer (1950) added a new dimension to the study of nail withdrawal strength. They studied the resistance to direct withdrawal of various types of nails driven into green and dry wood subjected to cycles of wetting and drying. Eight types of 7d nails (Fig. 2) were used to determine maximum static load and impact withdrawal energy from radial, tangential, and end grain in eastern white pine and southern yellow pine under various moisture conditions.

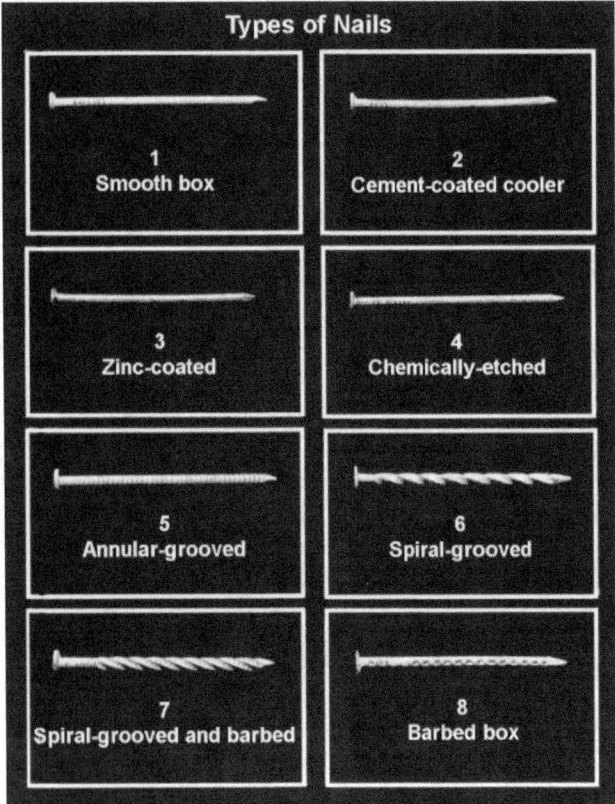

Figure 2—Different types of nails used by Borkenhagen and Heyer (1950).

Nails were driven through a 19.1-mm (0.75-in.) faceplate in three grain orientations; the faceplates were made from the same wood species as the specimens to simulate actual nailing practice. The nails were driven to a depth of 38 mm (1.5 in.) and withdrawn at a constant rate of 1.7 mm/min (0.07 in/min). No predrilled holes were used. Moisture conditions for fabrication and testing and applicable moisture cycling were as follows:

1. Driven in green material—pulled at once

2. Driven in dry material—pulled at once

3. Driven in green material—pulled after drying

4. Driven in green material—dried, wetted, dried, and pulled

5. Driven in dry material—wetted and pulled

6. Driven in green material—dried, wetted, dried, wetted, dried, and pulled

7. Driven in dry material—wetted, dried, and pulled

8. Driven in dry material—wetted, dried, wetted, dried, wetted, dried, and pulled

For each moisture cycle, nail type, and withdrawal orientation, 20 replicates were tested. Each replicate was derived

Figure 3—Impact withdrawal apparatus of Borkenhagen and Heyer (1950).

from a different board. The process of changing the specimen from a given moisture content to another moisture condition was consistent through the various cycles. The transition from dry to green was accomplished by submerging the individual test blocks in a tank of water and placing the tank in a sealed chamber to which mild pressure was applied for a limited time. An additional 2 days were required to permit the moisture to become uniformly distributed through the specimen. The transition from green to dry required considerably more time. Specimens were maintained under damp wraps and moved through a series of drying stages to prevent end checking, which is caused by rapidly changing moisture conditions.

Average static withdrawal load for each orientation and each nail type by wood species and moisture cycle are summarized in Tables 8 and 9 for nails driven into dry and green wood, respectively. The tables also provide the ratio of end- to side-grain withdrawal strength and average test moisture content.

For the impact tests, Borkenhagen and Heyer (1950) used a pendulum impact tester to determine the energy needed to withdraw nails driven into the radial, tangential, and end faces through a 19.1-mm (0.75-in.) faceplate (Fig. 3). A constant weight was released that impacted and withdrew the nail. The impact energy needed to withdraw the nail was determined based on the initial and final angles of the pendulum. The same types of nails, same species, and same moisture cycles were used for the impact tests as for static loading, except conditions 7 and 8 were dropped from the testing protocol. Table 10 summarizes the average impact withdrawal energy for each nail type, wood species, and moisture cycle protocol. Like Tables 8 and 9, Table 10 includes average test moisture content and the ratio of end- to side-grain withdrawal strength.

Table 8—Effects of moisture cycles on static withdrawal strength of fabricated dry specimens (Borkenhagen and Heyer 1950)

Nail type	Nail geometry (mm)		Mois-ture cycle	Test condition	Southern yellow pine				Eastern white pine			
	Diam.	Length			MC[a] (%)	Withdrawal load (N)		End/side ratio	MC (%)	Withdrawal load (N)		End/side ratio
						Side	End			Side	End	
Box	2.4	54.0	0	Dry	10.6	738	391	0.53	9.1	340	182	0.54
			0	Wet	58.2	560	245	0.44	72.6	258	120	0.47
			1	Dry	14.2	274	165	0.60	14.9	156	156	1.00
			3	Dry	14.8	681	343	0.50	13.5	374	196	0.52
Cement-coated	2.5	54.0	0	Dry	10.7	1,092	658	0.60	9.1	596	396	0.66
			0	Wet	59.1	781	338	0.43	76.8	414	249	0.60
			1	Dry	14.5	274	165	0.60	15.2	220	254	1.15
			3	Dry	14.9	469	205	0.44	13.7	358	222	0.62
Zinc-coated	2.6	54.0	0	Dry	10.8	1,246	667	0.54	9.3	434	267	0.62
			0	Wet	57.0	761	343	0.45	75.4	374	196	0.52
			1	Dry	14.2	418	476	1.14	15.1	189	267	1.41
			3	Dry	14.8	545	423	0.78	13.7	262	205	0.78
Chemically etched	2.5	54.0	0	Dry	10.9	1,076	716	0.67	9.3	474	343	0.72
			0	Wet	58.7	778	320	0.41	74.4	487	214	0.44
			1	Dry	14.2	438	405	0.92	14.7	334	294	0.88
			3	Dry	14.9	770	320	0.42	13.5	520	365	0.70
Annularly threaded	3.0	58.7	0	Dry	11.0	1,415	543	0.38	9.6	725	222	0.31
			0	Wet	59.6	1,110	387	0.35	76.3	634	214	0.34
			1	Dry	14.3	1,308	601	0.46	15.0	981	480	0.49
			3	Dry	14.9	1,788	685	0.38	13.7	1,286	596	0.46
Helically threaded	3.1	57.2	0	Dry	10.6	894	547	0.61	9.0	334	240	0.72
			0	Wet	59.1	723	280	0.39	74.7	343	133	0.39
			1	Dry	14.1	1,096	663	0.60	14.7	787	467	0.59
			3	Dry	14.8	1,181	801	0.68	13.4	1,014	641	0.63
Helically threaded, barbed	3.4	57.2	0	Dry	10.3	959	507	0.53	9.5	438	267	0.61
			0	Wet	59.9	827	294	0.35	76.6	465	178	0.38
			1	Dry	14.3	1,063	560	0.53	15.0	792	391	0.49
			3	Dry	14.9	1,659	685	0.41	13.6	1,165	614	0.53
Barbed	2.6	58.7	0	Dry	10.3	756	396	0.52	9.6	322	214	0.66
			0	Wet	59.0	534	178	0.33	76.0	271	102	0.38
			1	Dry	14.3	494	227	0.46	15.0	351	187	0.53
			3	Dry	14.8	781	365	0.47	13.6	554	276	0.50

[a] MC is moisture content.

Table 9—Effects of moisture cycle on static withdrawal strength of fabricated green specimens (Borkenhagen and Heyer 1950)

| Nail type | Nail geometry (mm) | | Mois-ture cycle | Test con-dition | Southern yellow pine | | | | Eastern white pine | | | |
	Diam.	Length			MC (%)	Withdrawal load (N) Side	End	End/side ratio	MC (%)	Withdrawal load (N) Side	End	End/side ratio
Box	2.4	54.0	0	Wet	52.5	939	431	0.46	81.1	403	196	0.49
			0	Dry	13.6	282	307	1.09	12.1	151	129	0.85
			1	Dry	14.5	222	178	0.80	15.1	180	151	0.84
			3	Dry	13.9	271	240	0.89	13.1	403	218	0.54
Cement-coated	2.5	54.0	0	Wet	55.8	1,014	445	0.44	81.6	576	267	0.46
			0	Dry	13.7	214	236	1.10	12.2	185	196	1.06
			1	Dry	14.4	331	169	0.51	15.2	191	160	0.84
			3	Dry	14.0	231	236	1.02	13.1	325	222	0.68
Zinc-coated	2.6	54.0	0	Wet	52.3	1,266	476	0.38	80.4	623	240	0.39
			0	Dry	13.8	529	552	1.04	12.0	222	365	1.64
			1	Dry	14.4	398	614	1.54	15.1	254	436	1.72
			3	Dry	14.0	349	676	1.94	12.9	383	454	1.19
Chemically etched	2.5	54.0	0	Wet	53.8	1,217	538	0.44	81.2	709	289	0.41
			0	Dry	13.8	480	498	1.04	12.0	345	458	1.33
			1	Dry	14.4	380	485	1.27	15.4	329	383	1.16
			3	Dry	14.0	398	520	1.31	12.9	609	516	0.85
Annularly threaded	3.0	58.7	0	Wet	52.7	1,539	494	0.32	80.9	785	205	0.26
			0	Dry	13.8	1,326	498	0.38	12.0	1,128	383	0.34
			1	Dry	14.4	1,455	485	0.33	15.4	1,252	458	0.37
			3	Dry	14.0	1,125	520	0.46	12.9	1,439	609	0.42
Helically threaded	3.1	57.2	0	Wet	54.9	1,014	463	0.46	80.7	447	147	0.33
			0	Dry	13.6	838	583	0.69	12.0	636	409	0.64
			1	Dry	14.4	1,034	867	0.84	15.7	859	463	0.54
			3	Dry	14.0	890	694	0.78	12.9	1,076	703	0.65
Helically threaded, barbed	3.4	57.2	0	Wet	53.2	1,110	476	0.43	80.6	507	258	0.51
			0	Dry	13.7	818	485	0.59	11.8	689	396	0.57
			1	Dry	14.7	1,246	658	0.53	15.3	916	552	0.60
			3	Dry	14.3	1,032	681	0.66	13.0	1,170	703	0.60
Barbed	2.6	58.7	0	Wet	52.6	865	351	0.41	80.4	396	160	0.40
			0	Dry	13.7	358	298	0.83	12.1	309	209	0.68
			1	Dry	14.6	409	289	0.71	14.9	423	236	0.56
			3	Dry	14.3	389	311	0.80	13.1	543	311	0.57

Table 10—Effects of moisture cycle on impact withdrawal strength (Borkenhagen and Heyer 1950)

| Nail type | Nail geometry (mm) | | Fabri-cation-condi-tion | Mois-ture cycle | Test con-dition | Southern yellow pine | | | | Eastern white pine | | | |
| | Diam. | Length | | | | MC (%) | Withdrawal load (N) | | End/side ratio | MC (%) | Withdrawal load (N) | | End/side ratio |
							Side	End			Side	End	
Box	2.4	54.0	Wet	0	Wet	52.5	13.45	4.79	0.36	81.1	9.32	4.29	0.46
				0	Dry	13.6	6.55	4.29	0.66	12.1	5.48	3.50	0.64
				1	Dry	14.5	6.84	3.39	0.50	15.1	6.44	4.18	0.65
				3	Dry	13.9	6.38	3.73	0.58	13.1	4.75	4.41	0.93
			Dry	0	Dry	10.6	14.69	7.91	0.54	9.1	8.76	4.97	0.57
				0	Wet	58.2	6.72	3.05	0.45	72.6	4.97	2.71	0.55
Cement-coated	2.5	54.0	Wet	0	Wet	55.8	13.84	6.33	0.46	81.6	11.24	4.86	0.43
				0	Dry	13.7	5.65	3.50	0.62	12.2	4.86	3.84	0.79
				1	Dry	14.4	5.54	3.50	0.63	15.2	5.76	4.07	0.71
				3	Dry	14.0	5.25	3.62	0.69	13.1	4.46	3.73	0.84
			Dry	0	Dry	10.7	16.27	11.07	0.68	9.1	9.21	5.76	0.63
				0	Wet	59.1	7.74	4.41	0.57	76.8	7.01	4.52	0.65
Zinc-coated	2.6	54.0	Wet	0	Wet	52.3	13.28	5.31	0.40	80.4	10.34	4.41	0.43
				0	Dry	13.8	8.19	5.76	0.70	12.0	5.48	3.84	0.70
				1	Dry	14.4	7.63	5.88	0.77	15.1	6.38	5.08	0.80
				3	Dry	14.0	6.89	5.76	0.84	12.9	4.58	4.63	1.01
			Dry	0	Dry	10.8	14.91	8.47	0.57	9.3	6.61	3.95	0.60
				0	Wet	57.0	6.95	3.39	0.49	75.4	5.93	3.50	0.59
Chemically etched	2.5	54.0	Wet	0	Wet	53.8	12.43	5.42	0.44	81.2	10.17	3.95	0.39
				0	Dry	13.8	6.95	4.18	0.60	12.0	5.76	4.75	0.82
				1	Dry	14.3	6.78	4.29	0.63	15.4	7.29	5.42	0.74
				3	Dry	14.1	6.16	5.20	0.84	12.9	5.08	4.97	0.98
			Dry	0	Dry	10.9	13.73	9.15	0.67	9.3	6.50	4.07	0.63
				0	Wet	58.7	6.27	3.05	0.49	74.4	5.82	3.28	0.56
Annularly threaded	3.0	58.7		0	Wet	52.7	13.61	5.88	0.43	80.9	8.87	4.86	0.55
				0	Dry	13.8	14.69	7.68	0.52	12.0	11.13	7.68	0.69
				1	Dry	14.4	17.06	8.81	0.52	15.4	13.90	9.49	0.68
				3	Dry	14.0	18.19	10.06	0.55	12.9	13.11	8.93	0.68
			Dry	0	Dry	11.0	13.33	8.81	0.66	9.6	6.44	4.29	0.67
				0	Wet	59.6	10.28	5.42	0.53	76.3	7.40	4.63	0.63
Helically threaded	3.1	57.2		0	Wet	54.9	13.33	6.55	0.49	80.7	8.87	5.20	0.59
				0	Dry	13.6	18.47	14.69	0.80	12.0	14.86	11.19	0.75
				1	Dry	14.4	17.91	15.03	0.84	15.7	16.95	12.77	0.75
				3	Dry	14.0	19.72	14.58	0.74	12.9	16.10	11.75	0.73
			Dry	0	Dry	10.6	19.21	11.19	0.58	9.0	9.89	5.99	0.61
				0	Wet	59.1	8.76	4.86	0.55	74.7	8.47	5.20	0.61
Helically threaded, barbed	3.4	57.2		0	Wet	53.2	15.93	8.59	0.54	80.6	10.96	7.01	0.64
				0	Dry	13.7	19.60	12.09	0.62	11.8	15.20	11.07	0.73
				1	Dry	14.7	21.47	14.69	0.68	15.3	18.30	13.56	0.74
				3	Dry	14.3	22.09	15.25	0.69	13.0	18.13	13.56	0.75
			Dry	0	Dry	10.3	17.91	11.98	0.67	9.5	10.06	7.34	0.73
				0	Wet	59.9	10.90	5.99	0.55	76.6	9.60	5.88	0.61
Barbed	2.6	58.7		0	Wet	52.6	11.13	4.18	0.38	80.4	8.08	3.62	0.45
				0	Dry	13.7	7.40	5.20	0.70	12.1	6.84	5.08	0.74
				1	Dry	14.5	7.74	4.97	0.64	14.9	8.08	5.88	0.73
				3	Dry	14.3	7.12	5.08	0.71	13.1	6.72	5.31	0.79
			Dry	0	Dry	10.3	13.45	7.80	0.58	9.6	7.23	4.63	0.64
				0	Wet	59.0	5.08	2.60	0.51	76.0	4.46	2.49	0.56

Table 11—End and side grain withdrawal load of different types and sizes of nails (Stern 1950)

Nail type	Nail geometry (mm)		Withdrawal load (N)		End/side strength ratio
	Diam.	Length	Side	End	
Plain	3.4	64	—	1,019	—
	4.1	89	—	1,726	—
	5.2	102	—	1,842	—
Helically threaded	3.4	64	1,539	1,299	0.84
	3.8	76	2,024	1,225	0.61
	4.1	89	—	2,131	—
	5.2	102	3,648	2,729	0.75
Annularly threaded	3.4	64	2,900	1,532	0.53
	3.8	76	4,155	1,584	0.38
	4.1	89	—	2,562	—
	5.2	102	6,419	3,200	0.50

Stern (1950) investigated the effects of different sizes of nails and different nail geometries on the holding power of nails in side- and end-grain lumber. Several sizes of plain, helically threaded, and annularly threaded nails were tested in Southern Pine end grain at different moisture content levels. Table 11 provides average results of five tests.

In 1970, Stern investigated the effectiveness of a new nail developed by Senco Products, Inc., of Cincinnati, Ohio. The head of this smooth shank nail was designed for use with a pneumatic hammer. Stern drove five types of nails into the side and end grain of 38-mm (1.5-in.) green Southern Pine and Red Oak. Matched assemblies were tested immediately after fabrication and after 6 weeks.

Moisture content immediately after fabrication ranged from 63% to 50% for Southern Pine assemblies and 77% to 59% for Red Oak assemblies. After 6 weeks, moisture content ranged from 11.7% to 11.5% for Southern Pine and 21.3% to 18.5% for Red Oak. Both static and impact withdrawal tests were conducted. Static tests followed ASTM 1761 procedures. Impact tests consisted of dropping a fixed weight from successively greater heights. For end-grain withdrawal tests, a 67-N (15-lbf) weight was dropped at increasing 12.1-mm (0.5-in.) increments, starting at a height of 12.1 mm (0.5-in.). For side-grain withdrawal tests, the same weight was dropped at increasing 51-mm (2-in.) increments, starting at a height of 51 mm (2 in.). The total nail withdrawal energy was calculated as the sum of the energy imparted by the weight over all the heights until the joint failed (Stern 1965).

End-to-end, side-to-side, and end-to-side delayed withdrawal strength ratios for the five nail types are presented for static and impact loading in Tables 12 and 13, respectively. Each test cell represents the average of 20 replicates.

Lhuede (1985) investigated the possibility of establishing end-grain design withdrawal loads for single nails. He conducted immediate, 2-day, 3-month, and 6-month static withdrawal tests of seven types of nails in five wood species. Specimens for delayed withdrawal tests were maintained at 20°C (68°F) and 65% relative humidity until testing. Moisture content of these fabricated green specimens was 12% to 20% after 3 months and 11.5% to 13% after 6 months or longer. Nails were driven by both hand and pneumatic gun to a depth of approximately 45 mm (1.75 in.) through a solid block into a predrilled hole in the mating block of the same species. Nails were withdrawn at rate such that the maximum load was achieved between 2 and 3 min.

Average end- and side-grain withdrawal loads per depth of penetration for various times, species, and nail types are shown in Tables 14 and 15 for dry and green specimens, respectively. Some experimental results were not reported because of limited data, lack of matching side-grain data, incomplete data for time intervals, or inadequate details about nail characteristics.

Two studies investigated the withdrawal performance of end-nailed joints. Scholten and Molander (1950) examined the lateral withdrawal strength of joints made by toenailing, end nailing, and using several types of metal fasteners. The end-nailed joint consisted of two nails, nailed through the side grain of a 38- by 89-mm (nominal 2- by 4-in.) board into the end grain of another 38- by 89-mm (nominal 2- by 4-in.) board using 10d (3.76-mm, 0.148-in.), 16d (4.11-mm, 0.162-in.), and 20d (4.88-mm, 0.19-in.) nails. Two-thirds of the specimens were fabricated from green and dry Douglas-fir and tested in the same condition. One-third were fabricated green and tested after drying. A withdrawal load was applied at a rate of 0.32 mm/min (0.0125 in/min).

The average results of the end-nailed joint withdrawal tests are presented for each test condition and nail size in Table 16. Characteristic load–slip curves for each type of joint are shown in Figure 4.

Whitney (1977) investigated the delayed withdrawal capacity of joints fabricated with nails driven into the end and side grain and slant-driven nails. Most tests were conducted on wet and dry radiata pine using 4.5 by 100-mm (0.17- by 3.94-in.) common nails. Some auxiliary joint tests were conducted using one nail and Corsican pine. A minimum of 12 replications were used for each test condition. Average maximum joint end-grain withdrawal capacity values are listed in Table 17.

Table 12—Effect of time delay on static nail withdrawal strength (Stern 1970)

Orientation comparison	Wood species [a]	Time [b]	Common (4.1×89 mm)	Smooth, box (3.5×89 mm)	Cement-coated (3.8×83 mm)	Uncoated Senco (3.2×89 mm)	Coated Senco (3.2×89 mm)
			Ratio of delayed to immediate withdrawal strength				
End to end	S. Pine	0 and 6 wk	0.59	0.67	0.58	0.50	1.07
	R. Oak	0 and 6 wk	0.68	0.83	0.50	0.75	0.77
Side to side	S. Pine	0 and 6 wk	0.29	0.29	0.25	0.22	0.48
	R. Oak	0 and 6 wk	0.6	0.61	0.45	0.59	0.6
			Ratio of end- to side-grain withdrawal strength				
End to side	S. Pine	0 wk	0.49	0.53	0.65	0.70	0.74
		6 wk	1.00	1.23	1.53	1.57	1.65
	R. Oak	0 wk	0.73	0.68	0.70	0.74	0.77
		6 wk	0.83	0.93	0.85	0.94	0.98

[a] S. Pine is Southern Pine; R. Oak, Red Oak.
[b] Assemblies tested immediately (0 weeks) and 6 weeks after fabrication.

Table 13—Effect of time delay on impact nail withdrawal strength (Stern 1970)

Orientation comparison	Wood species	Time	Common (4.1×89 mm)	Smooth, box (3.5×89 mm)	Cement-coated (3.8×83 mm)	Uncoated Senco (3.2×89 mm)	Coated Senco (3.2×89 mm)
			Ratio of delayed to immediate withdrawal strength				
End to end	S. Pine	0 and 6 wk	0.60	0.60	0.63	0.56	0.71
	R. Oak	0 and 6 wk	0.53	0.59	0.37	0.54	0.85
Side to side	S. Pine	0 and 6 wk	0.45	0.59	0.42	0.23	0.19
	R. Oak	0 and 6 wk	0.41	0.46	0.38	0.42	0.25
			Ratio of end- to side-grain withdrawal strength				
End to side	S. Pine	0 wk	0.49	0.44	0.46	0.28	0.24
		6 wk	0.66	0.45	0.70	0.70	0.86
	R. Oak	0 wk	0.63	0.51	0.49	0.42	0.25
		6 wk	0.81	0.66	0.48	0.54	0.85

Discussion

Based on a large body of information on side-grain withdrawal strength, withdrawal strength is known to be a function of fastener penetration, fastener diameter, specific gravity, and moisture content as well as other factors. Common observations are presented for these parameters across various studies. The sections on specific gravity and the end-to side-grain withdrawal ratio focus on immediate end-grain withdrawal performance. The sections on time effects and moisture cycling discuss longer term end-grain withdrawal performance. Additionally, the effect of impact withdrawal is briefly discussed.

Table 14—Static withdrawal loads for nails driven into dry wood and tested at various intervals (Lhuede 1985)

Wood species	Moisture content (%)	Specific gravity	Nail type	Nail diam. (mm)	Driving method	Immediate End	Immediate Side	2 days End	2 days Side	3 months End	3 months Side	6 months End	6 months Side
Jarrah	12.0	0.648	Plain	3.15	Hand	75.1	93.7	59.9	—	48.4	67.7	48.7	69.1
			Plain	3.05	Machine	92.9	135.0	—	—	69.6	87.3	—	—
			Annular	3.05	Machine	120.3	156.9	99.3	150.9	91.2	—	87.5	132.0
			Helical	3.05	Machine	108.7	136.2	101.8	123.7	83.8	122.3	86.9	110.6
Mountain ash	11.8	0.475	Plain	3.15	Hand	30.7	37.8	23.4	—	16.4	27.4	16.0	27.9
			Plain	3.05	Machine	37.6	63.0	-	39.0	55.8	—	—	—
			Annular	3.05	Machine	49.7	80.3	40.8	81.4	38.0	—	37.2	74.9
			Helical	3.05	Machine	38.8	58.3	33.5	51.5	34.5	46.7	29.9	43.8
Radiata pine	10.2	0.437	Plain	3.15	Hand	19.3	24.2	17.0	—	16.5	23.4	17.4	21.4
			Plain	3.05	Machine	36.6	51.9	—	—	—	47.4	—	—
			Annular	3.05	Machine	44.0	64.4	34.0	62.6	36.0	—	31.7	50.8
			Helical	3.05	Machine	36.6	46.7	31.1	48.1	27.8	43.2	27.2	38.5

Table 15—Static withdrawal loads for nails driven into green wood and tested at various intervals (Lhuede 1985)

Wood species	Moisture content (%)	Specific gravity	Nail type	Nail diam. (mm)	Driving method	Immediate End	Immediate Side	2 days End	2 days Side	3 months End	3 months Side	6 months End	6 months Side
Jarrah	70.1	0.648	Plain	3.15	Hand	43.4	66.6	44.4	—	27.8	23.6	28.1	24.9
			Plain	3.05	Machine	38.7	50.5	—	—	21.6	18.2	—	—
			Annular	3.05	Machine	45.5	62.0	45.5	65.2	50.1	—	55.5	54.4
			Helical	3.05	Machine	51.1	67.5	57.5	71.3	63.0	81.6	63.9	86.7
Messmate	79.0	0.475	Plain	3.15	Hand	40.8	69.4	39.0	—	20.9	30.6	23.4	26.0
			Plain	3.05	Machine	31.7	47.3	—	—	23.9	18.8	—	—
			Annular	3.05	Machine	39.2	62.4	36.1	54.3	34.6	—	31.2	49.3
			Helical	3.05	Machine	45.1	71.1	46.5	68.0	38.6	71.5	40.8	67.1

Table 16—Strength of end-nailed joints (Scholten and Molander 1950)

Nails Size	No.	Joints fabricated dry, tested dry — Load at 0.38-mm slip (N)	Maximum Load (N)	Maximum Slip (mm)	Joints fabricated green, tested green — Load at 0.38-mm slip (N)	Maximum Load (N)	Maximum Slip (mm)	Joints fabricated green, tested dry — Load at 0.38-mm slip (N)	Maximum Load (N)	Maximum Slip (mm)
10d	2	—	1,379	0.5	—	996	0.25	463	569	3.3
16d	2	—	939	0.25	—	1,539	0.25	618	725	6.9
20d	2	2,220	2,304	0.5	—	2,638	0.25	738	1,001	11.0

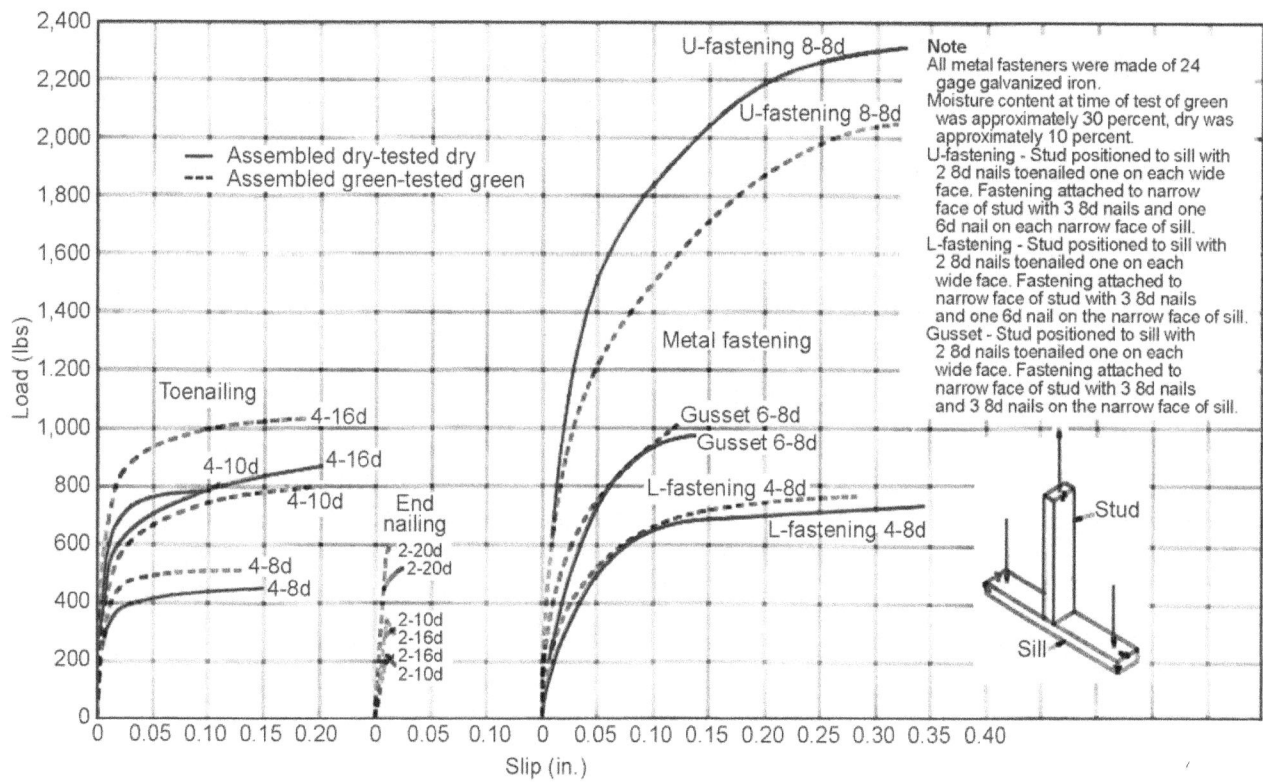

Figure 4—Load–slip curves for different types of wood fasteners. (Scholten and Molander 1950)

Table 17—Strength of delayed withdrawal end-nailed joints (Whitney 1977)

Wood species	Nail diameter (mm)	No. of joints	No. of specimens	Specific gravity	Maximum delayed withdrawal load (kN)			
					Average		Predicted	
					Dry	Green	Dry	Green
Radiata pine	4.5	2	27	0.44	2.19	2.15	2.15	1.37
Corsican pine	4.5	2	20	0.42	1.81	1.88	2.00	1.27
Corsican pine	4.5	1	20	0.42	1.11	0.78	1.00	0.64

Specific Gravity Effects

Wood species with high specific gravity have high nail-holding power in both the side and end grain. To determine how nail-holding power varies with specific gravity for nails driven into the end grain and withdrawn immediately, five data sets were combined and weighted according to the number of replicates for a given nail type and wood species. A total of 4,723 data points were used: 4,388 from Gahagan and Scholten (1938), 40 from Borkenhagen and Heyer (1950) 15 from Stern (1950), 10 from Stern (1970), and 270 from Lhuede (1985). Data from the studies by Langlands (1933) and Huston (1947) were not included in the analysis because they lacked specific gravity values. A best-fit power curve of the form

$$W = adg^{b} \qquad (2)$$

was then calculated, where

W is load (N) divided by nail penetration depth (mm),
d is nail diameter (mm),
g is specific gravity (oven-dry weight and volume at time of test), and
a, b are empirical constants to be determined.

This equation form has historically been utilized to evaluate fastener withdrawal from wood material and was the only form considered here (Forest Product Laboratory 1999, McLain 1997, Rammer and others 2001).

Using a Markquardt–Levenberg nonlinear curve fitting procedure, we found that the best fit of a and b to the data set was 21.73 N/mm^2 and 1.75, respectively. Plots revealed that Lheude's (1985) results for Jarrah were significantly higher than the remaining data trend, so we chose to remove that set for further analysis. Elimination of this data set resulted in a conservative relationship. Analyzing the new data set resulted in $a = 17.65$ N/mm^2 and $b = 1.52$.

Since the coefficient b is similar to the 3/2 factor used for immediate side-grain withdrawal, the final expression was determined by setting $b = 3/2$. Re-analyzing to determine a, the immediate withdrawal strength per depth of penetration into the end grain for a common nail can be expressed as

$$W = 17.45 dg^{3/2} \qquad (3)$$

If expressed in inch–pound units (lbf/in^2), $a = 2{,}531$ lbf/in^2. This equation had a coefficient of determination (r^2) of 0.54 for the data set considered.

McLain (1997) compared various curve fits to the immediate withdrawal strength of nails driven into the side grain by comparing the values of the mean percentage deviation (MD)

$$MD = \frac{\sum_{i=1}^{n} \left[\dfrac{y_i - \hat{y}(g_i, d_i)}{\hat{y}(g_i, d_i)} \right] \cdot 100}{n} \qquad (4)$$

and standard error of estimate (SEE)

$$SEE = \sqrt{\frac{\sum_{i=1}^{n} \left[\dfrac{y_i - \hat{y}(g_i, d_i) \cdot 100}{\hat{y}(g_i, d_i)} \right]^2}{n-1}} \qquad (5)$$

where y_i is the ith observed withdrawal strength, $\hat{y}(g_i, d_i)$ is the predicted withdrawal strength for the given specific gravity and nail diameter for the ith specimen, and n is the total number of data points.

To evaluate the effectiveness of the immediate end-grain withdrawal expression (Eq. (3)), the MD and SEE statistics for both Equation (3) and the immediate side-grain withdrawal expression (Eq. (2)), were calculated using the five matched data sets. The MD and SEE for the immediate side-grain withdrawal strength were 16.1% and 35.2%, respectively; for the immediate end-grain withdrawal strength, MD was 0.69% and SEE was 31.9%. The immediate end-grain withdrawal strength statistics were similar to those for the immediate side-grain withdrawal strength. Therefore, we can state that Equation (3) predicts the immediate withdrawal strength of nails driven into the end grain to the same level of accuracy as does Equation (2), the expression from which the current design values for side-grain withdrawal are based.

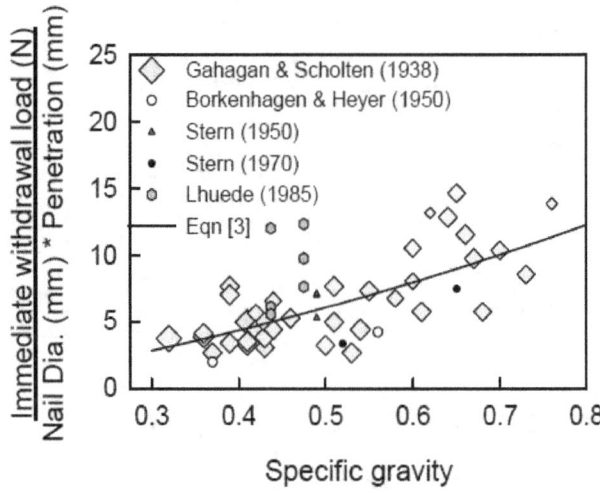

Figure 5—Relationship between immediate withdrawal strength and specific gravity for combined data set.

Finally, moving the depth of penetration to the other side of the expression yields the following equation:

$$P = aLdg^{3/2} \qquad (6)$$

where

P is   immediate end-grain withdrawal strength, N (lbf),

a an empirical constant, 17.45 N/mm^2 (2,531 lbf/in^2),

L nail penetration depth, mm (in.),

d nail diameter, mm (in.), and

g specific gravity based on oven-dry weight and wet volume.

End-grain withdrawal strength values of common nails for the five data sets and Equation (3) are plotted as a function of specific gravity in Figure 5. The size of the symbol indicates the relative size of the data set at a given specific gravity. As Figure 5 shows, Equation (3) adequately predicts the withdrawal performance of smooth nails from dry end grain.

Immediate End- to Side-Grain Withdrawal Strength Ratio

As stated in the Introduction to this report, the *Wood Handbook* (Forest Products Laboratory 1999) declares

> when the nail is driven parallel to the wood fibers… withdrawal resistance drops to 75% or even 50% of the resistance obtained when the nail is driven perpendicular to the grain…

To examine the validity of this statement, we calculated the ratio of immediate end- to side-grain withdrawal strength from the experimental data generated in the previously discussed studies. Immediate side-grain withdrawal strength was calculated as the average of radial and tangential withdrawal strengths.

16

Langlands (1933) tested a wide range of nails in both the end and side grain. For the two common nails tested, the immediate withdrawal side- to end-grain ratios were 0.50 and 0.53. For all the remaining types of nails tested, the ratios varied between 0.65 and 0.47, with the minimum ratio corresponding to the withdrawal strength of rusted common nails.

In tests by Gahagan and Scholten (1938), immediate side- to end-grain withdrawal ratios for common nails varied from a maximum of 0.80, for Engelmann spruce, to a minimum of 0.47, for virgin redwood, with an average ratio of 0.66 for all species (Table 4). Similar immediate withdrawal ratios were found for cement-coated nails. These ratios varied from a low of 0.36 for lowland white pine to a high of 1.00 for black locust, with an average ratio of 0.65 for all species tested (Table 5).

Based on Huston's data for plain nails (Huston 1947), the calculated immediate end- to side-grain withdrawal strength ratio is 0.69 in eastern white pine and 0.61 in southern yellow pine. For cement-coated nails, the calculated end- to side-grain strength ratio is 0.59 in eastern white pine and 0.67 in southern yellow pine. These ratios are consistent with Gahagan and Scholten's work. In both species, the ratio of immediate end- to side-grain withdrawal strength was higher in specimens that were driven through a faceplate.

Borkenhagen and Heyer (1950) investigated the end- to side-grain withdrawal strength ratio across eight nail types and at two moisture content levels. The end- to side-grain withdrawal ratios for all nail types, both moisture content levels, and both wood species are shown in Figure 6. For box and cement-coated nails driven into and immediately withdrawn from dry Southern Pine, the ratios were 0.53 and 0.60, respectively. For dry eastern white pine, the immediate withdrawal ratios were 0.54 for box nails and 0.66 for cement-coated nails. All other nail types, except for the annularly threaded nails, had similar immediate end- to side-grain withdrawal strength ratios for dry wood, ranging from 0.53 to 0.72 with an arithmetic mean of 0.62.

Immediate withdrawal ratios for annularly threaded nails were 0.38 and 0.31 for Southern Pine and eastern white pine, respectively. In general, the end-grain withdrawal strength values were similar for all nail types; the lower ratio of the annularly threaded nail is attributed to the superior side-grain withdrawal strength of this type of nail.

In all cases, the immediate end- to side-grain withdrawal ratios for green specimens were lower than those for dry specimens; annularly threaded nails had the lowest ratio.

Stern (1950) tested three diameters of helically and annularly threaded nails in both side- and end-grain withdrawal in Southern Pine (Table 11). The immediate end- to side-grain withdrawal ratios ranged between 0.61 and 0.84 for helically threaded nails and between 0.38 and 0.53 for annularly threaded nails. Ratios for the helically threaded nails were

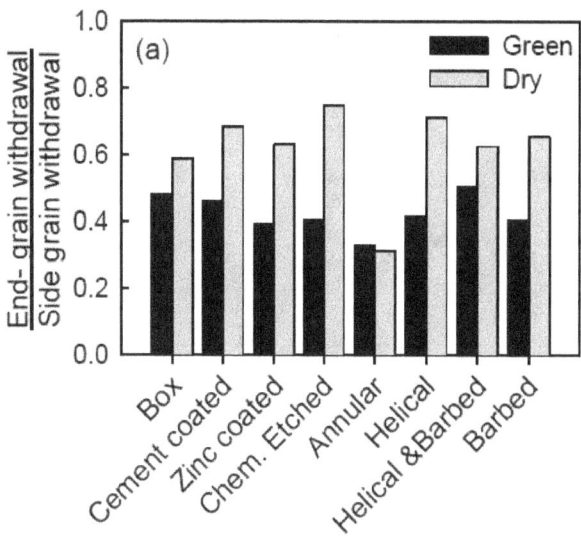

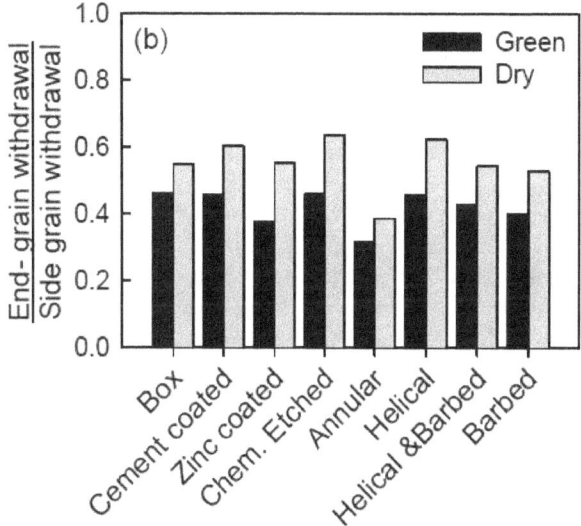

Figure 6—Immediate end- to side-grain withdrawal strength ratios for various nail types and two species of green and dry wood: (a) eastern white pine, (b) southern yellow pine. (Borkenhagen and Heyer 1950)

similar to those found by Borkenhagan and Heyer (1950), whereas ratios for the 3.4-mm (0.13-in.) and 5.2-mm (0.2-in.) annularly threaded nails were different from the ratio for the 3.8-mm (0.14-in.) annularly threaded nails and from the ratio found by Borkenhagan and Heyer.

The Senco nail research by Stern (1970) determined the withdrawal strength of five types of nails from the side and end grain of green Red Oak and Southern Pine (Table 12). For all nail types, immediate end- to side-grain withdrawal ratios ranged between 0.49 and 0.74 for Southern Pine and between 0.68 and 0.77 for Red Oak. All these ratios are similar to values found by other researchers (Gahagan and Scholten 1938, Borkenhagan and Heyer 1950).

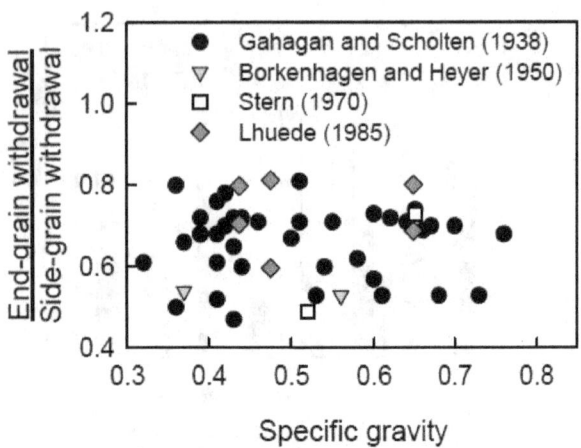

Figure 7—Immediate end- to side-grain withdrawal strength ratio for dry specimens as a function of specific gravity.

In the work by Lhuede (1985), immediate end- to side-grain withdrawal ratios for plain nails in three species of dry wood ranged between 0.60 and 0.81, with an average ratio of 0.73. For annularly threaded nails, the ratio for dry wood was between 0.62 and 0.77, whereas that for helically threaded nails was between 0.66 and 0.80. Ratios for the smooth and helically threaded nails are similar to ratios determined by other researchers. The end- to side-grain withdrawal ratio for the annularly threaded nails was higher than that found in previous studies. However, Lhuede's results may have been influenced by the surface coating on the annularly threaded nails.

To investigate how the immediate end- to side-grain withdrawal strength ratio for dry wood changes with specific gravity, the end- to side-grain ratios for smooth shank nails driven into dry wood were plotted as a function of specific gravity (Fig. 7). As Figure 7 indicates, the immediate end- to side-grain withdrawal ratio ranges between 0.80 and 0.50 and the ratio is independent of specific gravity. The independence of specific gravity, as shown in Figure 7, is inconsistent with the statement in the *Wood Handbook* that "the difference between end- to side-grain withdrawal loads is less for dense wood."

Across all studies, the immediate end- to side-grain withdrawal ratio ranged between 0.47 and 0.80 for common nails. These values are in line with the 75% to 50% ratio specified in the *Wood Handbook*, which was likely based on Gahagan and Scholten's original work. Based on the Borkenhagen and Heyer data, the ratio seems consistent across nail types except for the annularly threaded nail, which has a lower ratio because of its higher side-grain withdrawal value. Finally, the research shows that the immediate end- to side-grain withdrawal ratio is independent of specific gravity, which means the absolute difference between end- and side-grain withdrawal loads increases with specific gravity.

Time Effects

The statement in the *Wood Handbook* on delayed end-grain nail withdrawal strength addresses the effects of time and moisture content:

> With most species the ratio between the end- and side-grain withdrawal loads of nails pulled after a time interval, or after moisture changes have occurred, is usually somewhat higher than that of nails pulled immediately after driving.

This statement indicates that moisture changes or time delays increase the end- to side-grain withdrawal ratio or, stated differently, the difference between the end-grain and side-grain withdrawal load decreases.

Gahagan and Scholten (1938) and Lhuede (1985) investigated time effects, without a change in moisture content, on end-grain nail withdrawal strength. In comparing immediate withdrawal strength to withdrawal strength after 40 days and after 105 days, Gahagan and Scholten (1938) showed that both side- and end-grain withdrawal strength decreased over time when nails were driven into green material that was then allowed to dry. The rate of decrease was greatest in the side-grain withdrawal strength values, resulting in high end-to side-grain ratios after 40 and 105 days (Table 6). For ponderosa pine specimens fabricated and tested dry, both side- and end-grain withdrawal strength increased over time. For Southern Pine, side-grain withdrawal strength decreased over time but end-grain withdrawal strength was relatively constant. For both species, the end- to side-grain ratio was greater for the delayed tests than in immediate withdrawal tests. In all cases, the difference between the end-grain and side-grain withdrawal loads decreased with an increase in the time between fabrication and testing, compared with the results from the immediate withdrawal test.

Lhuede (1985) conducted both end- and side-grain withdrawal tests 2 h, 2 days, 3 months, and 6 months after specimen fabrication. Figure 8 shows the ratio of delayed end-grain withdrawal load to immediate withdrawal load and the ratio of end- to side-grain withdrawal load at each interval for the 3.15-mm (0.12-in.) common nail for three wood species. In general, the ratios decreased quickly, but the loss of end-grain withdrawal strength stabilized after 3 months. The decrease was greatest for the material with the highest specific gravity. Over the same intervals, the ratio of end- to side-grain withdrawal load was slightly lower than the ratio of delayed to immediate withdrawal load.

In Lhuede's study, end-grain withdrawal strength decreased over time, as did side-grain withdrawal strength. However, the effect of time on the end- to side-grain withdrawal strength ratio is not clear. For radiata pine the ratio tended to increase over time, whereas for Jarrah and mountain-ash the ratio decreased.

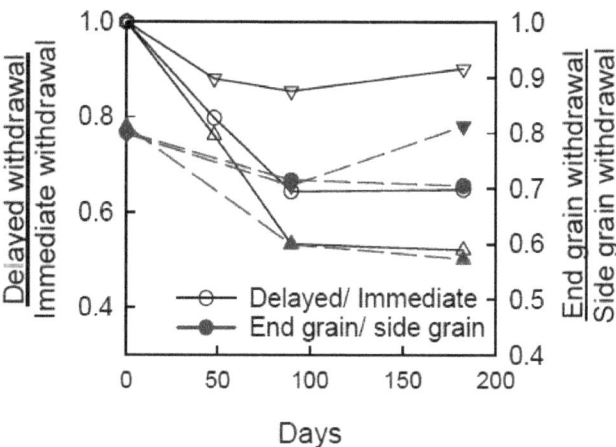

Figure 8—Delayed to immediate end-grain and end- to side-grain withdrawal ratios as a function of time for Jarrah, mountain-ash, and radiata pine. (Lhuede 1985)

Moisture Content Effects

The effects of changes in moisture content and time after fabrication are intertwined, since drying or wetting wood does not change its level of moisture content instantaneously. According to the *Wood Handbook*, the end- to side-grain withdrawal strength ratio increases after a change in moisture content. Borkenhagen and Heyer (1950), Langlands (1933), Gahagen and Scholten (1938), Stern (1970), and Lhuede (1985) investigated the effect of moisture content change on nail-holding power.

Borkenhagen and Heyer (1950) studied the static withdrawal strength of eight types of nails that were driven into both the end and side grain and were subjected to eight moisture change protocols. Results are shown only for the box, zinc-coated, annularly threaded, and helically threaded nails, nail types that are currently utilized in today's construction. Similar graphs could be generated for the remaining nail types from the information given in Tables 8 and 9. Furthermore, trends observed for these four nail types are similar to trends seen for the other types.

Figure 9 shows average static end-grain withdrawal strength as a function of the number of moisture cycles for box, zinc-coated, annularly threaded, and helically threaded nails. One moisture cycle is defined as dry to wet to dry; a half-cycle is defined as fabricated green to tested dry. For example, for 1-1/2 cycles, a specimen was fabricated green, dried, re-saturated, and dried again. The nail was then withdrawn. All cycles ended with a nail withdrawal test on dry wood. In Figure 9 and similar figures, variability is denoted by error bars, which represent one standard deviation to either side of the mean.

The end-grain withdrawal strength of the box nails and the zinc-coated nails fluctuated with the number of moisture cycles, but overall there is no obvious significant upward or downward trend. However, the zinc-coated nails showed more variability than the box nails. The end-grain withdrawal strength of both the annularly and helically threaded fasteners increased after cycles of wetting and drying. This increase was more pronounced in eastern white pine compared with southern yellow pine. Variability of end-grain withdrawal strength was greater for threaded nails than for box nails in similar wood specimens.

The withdrawal strength of side-grain nails subjected to cycles of wetting and drying mimics the response of the end-grain nails except for a significant drop in side-grain withdrawal strength after the first cycle for the box nails (Fig. 10). However, threaded nails maintained their side-grain withdrawal strength throughout the moisture cycles as they did when driven into the end grain. Representative average side-grain withdrawal strength as a function of moisture cycle is shown in Figure 10 for box and annularly threaded nails.

The *Wood Handbook* addresses changes in the ratio of end- to side-grain withdrawal strength. To evaluate the statement in the *Wood Handbook*, the average end- to side-grain static withdrawal ratio was plotted against the number of moisture cycles (Fig. 11). These data reveal the differences between the end- to side-grain withdrawal ratios of box and zinc-coated nails compared with that of threaded nails.

The bright box and zinc-coated nails tend to have higher variances across all moisture cycles. There appears to be no general monotonically increasing or decreasing trend for moisture cycling for the end- to side-grain withdrawal ratio. However, the ratio tends to be greater after moisture cycling compared to that immediately after withdrawal. Most of the increase in ratio occurs between the immediate and three-cycle conditions. The immediate and three-cycle end-to-side grain withdrawal ratios are visually similar for box and zinc-coated nails. For some conditions, the ratio indicates that end-grain withdrawal strength was greater than side-grain withdrawal strength, especially for the zinc-coated fastener.

By comparison, threaded fasteners tend to have a constant mean end- to side-grain withdrawal ratio throughout the cycles of wetting and drying. Furthermore, at any given moisture cycle, the threaded fasteners tend to have lower variances when compared to bright box and zinc-coated fasteners.

Langlands (1933) conducted studies that included both a 3-month interval and moderate changes in moisture content for 8 different nail types. In all cases, delayed withdrawal load was lower than immediate withdrawal load. The ratio of delayed to immediate withdrawal load varied between 0.44 and 1.02, with an average value of 0.67. Comparing the immediate and delayed ratios across all nail types (Table 2), 14 of the 21 delayed end- to side-grain withdrawal ratios increased or were constant. A similar change was observed in side-grain withdrawal strength over the

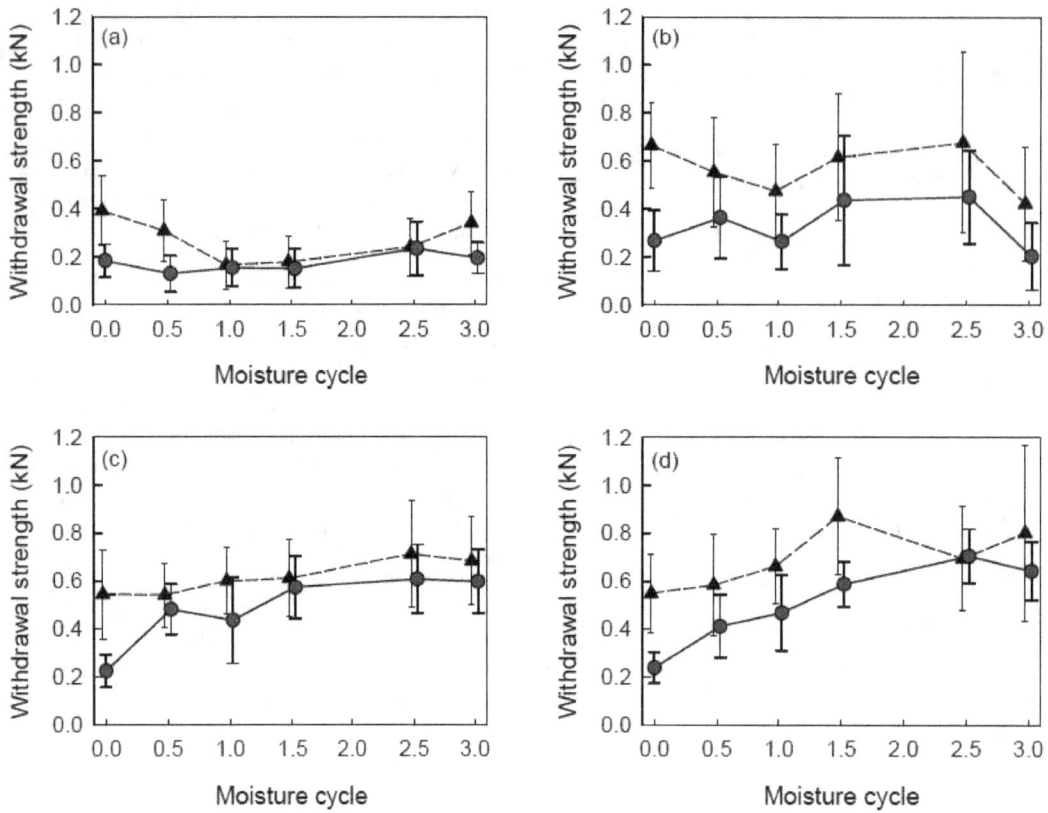

Figure 9—Static end-grain nail withdrawal strength in eastern white pine (circles) and southern yellow pine (triangles) for four nail types: (a) box, (b) zinc-coated, (c) annularly threaded, and (d) helically threaded. (Borkenhagen and Heyer 1950)

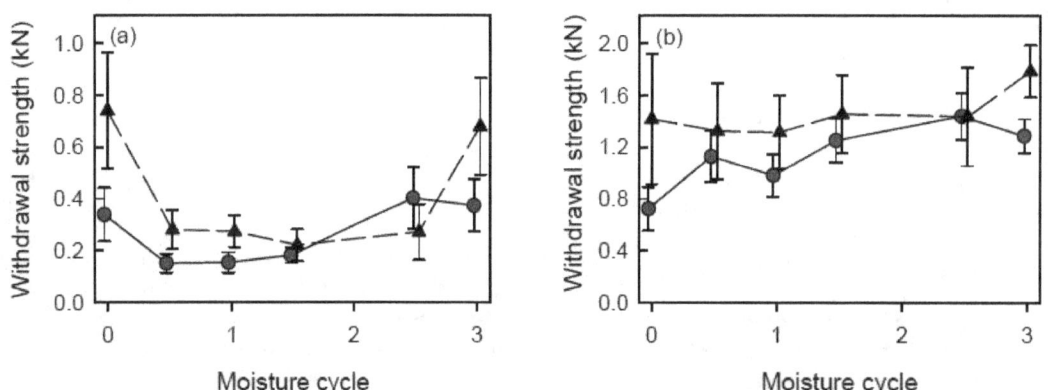

Figure 10—Static side-grain nail withdrawal strength in eastern white pine (circles) and southern yellow pine (triangles) for (a) box nails and (b) annularly threaded nails. (Borkenhagen and Heyer 1950)

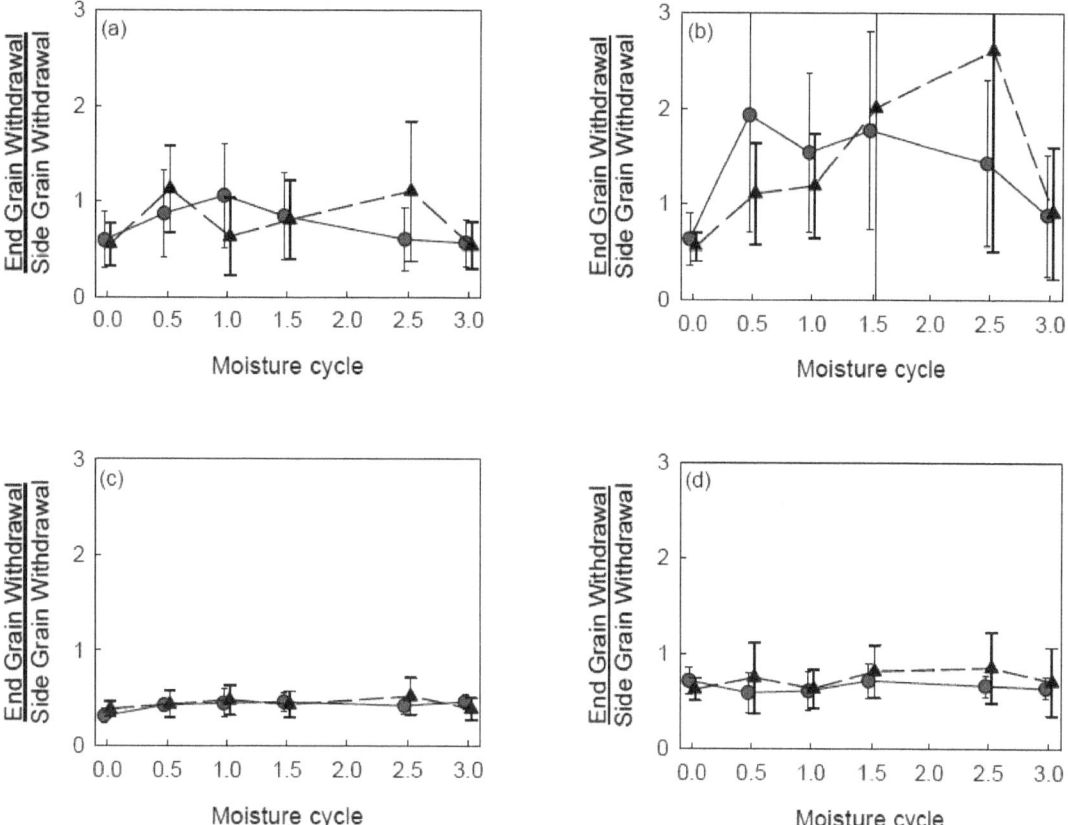

Figure 11—Effect of moisture cycles on static end- to side-grain withdrawal strength ratio for different nail types in eastern white pine (circles) and southern yellow pine (triangles): (a) box, (b) zinc-coated, (c) annularly threaded, and (d) helically threaded. (Borkenhagen and Heyer 1950)

3-month interval; in 14 cases, the immediate to delayed side-grain withdrawal ratio was smaller than the ratio for matching end-grain.

As part of Scholten and Gahagan's (1938) research on time effects, specimens were nailed green and allowed to dry for 40 and 105 days (Table 6). After 40 days, the end- to side-grain withdrawal ratios were 0.91 and 0.74 for ponderosa pine and Southern Pine, respectively; after 105 days, the end- to side-grain ratios were 1.60 and 0.69 for these species. For both time periods, the delayed end- to side-grain withdrawal ratio was greater than the immediate ratio.

Stern (1970) determined the immediate and 6-week delayed static withdrawal strength for five nail types driven into green wood and allowed to air dry (Table 12). None of the five fasteners was threaded. The ratio of delayed to immediate withdrawal strength indicated that both end-grain and side-grain withdrawal capacity decreased with a combination of time and drying. In all cases, the lowest delayed to immediate withdrawal ratios were recorded for nails driven into side grain. This indicates that the end- to side-grain withdrawal strength ratio would increase over time.

For all nails and both species in Stern's study (1970), the immediate end- to side-grain withdrawal ratios were between 0.49 and 0.74, similar to values found in other studies. All the delayed end- to side-grain withdrawal ratios increased with comparison to the immediate withdrawal ratios for matched specimens. This increase was more significant for nails withdrawn from Southern Pine. The data indicate that over time and with decrease in moisture content, the end-grain withdrawal capacity decreased at a slower rate than did the side-grain capacity; therefore the difference between end-grain and side-grain withdrawal capacity decreased.

Lhuede (1985) drove smooth annularly threaded and helically threaded nails into green Messmate and Jarrah and allowed the specimens to condition at 20°C (68°F) and 65% relative humidity for 2 days, 3 months, and 6 months. For the smooth 3.15-mm- (0.125-in.-) diameter nails, the end- to side-grain withdrawal ratio increased from an immediate value of 0.59 to 0.9 after 6 months in Messmate and from 0.65 to 1.13 in Jarrah. Lhuede also recorded the occurrence of critical splits in the specimen at the time of testing.

For the Messmate specimens, six end-grain and four side-grain splits were visible after 3 months, and eight end-grain and seven side-grain splits were present after 6 months. For Jarrah, only two end-grain splits and one side-grain split were noted after 3 months. Calculating a withdrawal capacity for the specimen containing splits, Lhuede found that splits decreased the withdrawal capacity by only 10%. For both annularly and helically threaded nails, the end- to side-grain withdrawal ratio was relativity constant for all times, with one exception: after 6 months, the withdrawal ratio for annularly threaded nails in Jarrah had increased to 1.02.

In summary, after cycles of wetting and drying, end-grain withdrawal values are constant or tend to increase slightly for threaded fasteners, whereas the withdrawal strength of box and surface-coated nails does not show any clear trend. Threaded fasteners tend to maintain their immediate end- to side-grain ratio, even after several cycles of wetting and drying, and have much lower variances than do the box or surface-coated nails. Smooth shank nails independent of coating type tend to have end- to side-grain ratios that are constant or increase with moisture cycles and time. In other words, for smooth shank fasteners, the difference between end- and side-grain withdrawal capacity decreases if the ratio increases.

Finally, the previous sections on time and moisture effects provide the foundation for the statement in the *Wood Handbook* about long-term changes in the end- to side-grain nail withdrawal strength ratio. That statement is likely based on the work of Gahagan and Scholten (1938) and Borkenhagen and Heyer (1950).

Nail Size Effects

Very few studies have tested the withdrawal strength of large nails driven into the end grain (Stern 1950, 1970). Figure 12 plots the ratio of immediate end-grain withdrawal strength for a given fastener diameter to immediate end-grain withdrawal strength of a 4.11-mm- (0.162-in.-) diameter smooth shank nail driven into Southern Pine and Red Oak. For the limited data plotted in Figure 12, larger nail diameters typically have greater immediate end-grain withdrawal strength. Figure 12 also includes the ratio of the radius squared of a 4.11-mm- (0.162-in.-) diameter smooth nail and the ratio of the nail radius. The change in immediate end-grain withdrawal strength is apparently directly related to the change in the ratio of the nail radius (diameter). More research is needed to define the influence of radius and depth of penetration. At present, we can assume that immediate end-grain withdrawal strength varies in proportion to nail diameter and depth of penetration.

Nail Surface Characteristics

For nails driven into the side grain of wood, research has shown that the immediate withdrawal strength of threaded nails is significantly greater than that of smooth shank nails of a similar size (Rammer and others 2001). This increase is attributed to the lodging of fibers between the threads. When threaded nails are driven into end grain, the lack of lodged fibers could reduce the effectiveness of the threads. Langlands (1933), Borkenhagen and Heyer (1950), Stern (1950), and Lhuede (1985) tested the effectiveness of different types of nails withdrawn from the end grain of wood.

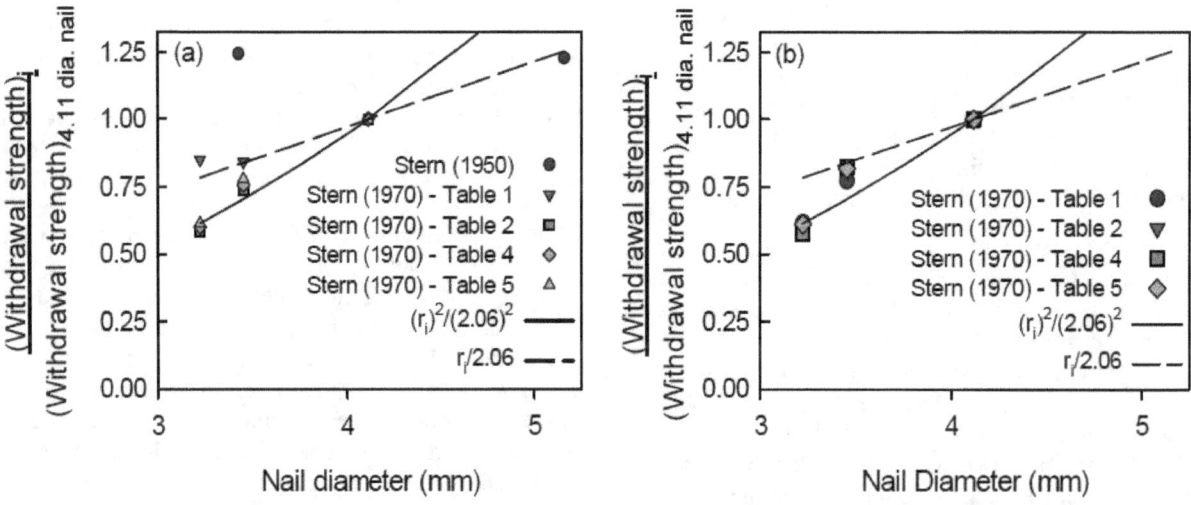

Figure 12—Ratio of immediate end-grain withdrawal strength for a given fastener diameter to that of a 4.11-mm-diameter smooth shank nail for (a) Southern Pine and (b) Red Oak. (Stern 1950, 1970)

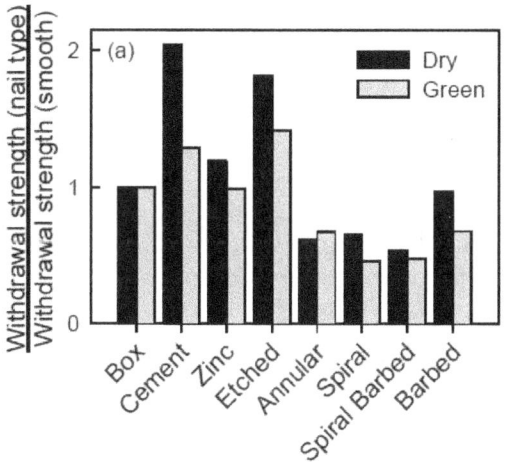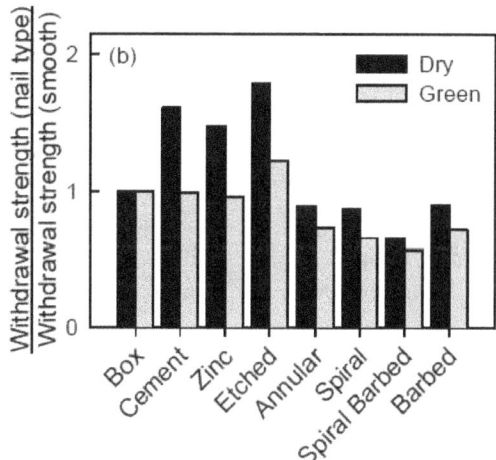

Figure 13—Ratio of immediate end-grain withdrawal strength for bright box nails to that for different nail types, adjusted to 2.51-mm diameter, for (a) eastern white pine and (b) southern yellow pine. (Borkenhagen and Heyer 1950)

Langlands (1933) tested eight different types of surface treatments for nails, but since their diameter varied and details on the fasteners were lacking, only general observations are noted here. Based on the combined end- and side-grain performance, Langlands concluded that nail surface characteristics have little impact on immediate withdrawal strength. After a 3-month delay, only the twisted nails (both uncoated and cement-coated) showed significantly greater withdrawal capacity than the other nail types.

Borkenhagan and Heyer (1950) tested the immediate withdrawal strength of eight nail types in green and dry Southern Pine and eastern white pine. The nails utilized in this study were not selected to have a similar diameter, so a direct comparison of nails cannot be made. Diameter ranged from 2.51 mm (0.099 in.) for a smooth shank nail to 3.41 mm (0.135 in.) for a barbed nail. To compare the effect of surface characteristics, the immediate withdrawal strength values were adjusted based on the proportion of nail diameter. To remove the influence of wood species and moisture content, the ratio of immediate end-grain withdrawal strength for box nails to that for a specific nail type was calculated.

Figure 13 shows the immediate end-grain withdrawal strength for each nail type normalized to that of a smooth shank nail in eastern white pine and Southern Pine in both the dry and green condition. Figure 13 indicates that the initial performance of coated and etched nails was the same as that of a smooth shank nail in green wood and exceeded smooth shank performance in dry wood. However, the withdrawal strength of threaded and barbed nails was generally lower than that of a smooth shank nail regardless of moisture condition. These nails were less effective in eastern white pine, which has a lower specific gravity than that of Southern Pine.

On the other hand, the data for Stern (1950) indicate that the end-grain withdrawal strength of annularly and helically threaded nails is greater than that of smooth shank nails of a similar size (Table 11). Stern concluded that even in end-grain Southern Pine grooved nails offer considerably greater withdrawal resistance than do plain shank nails.

Lhuede (1985) tested the withdrawal strength of plain, coated, annularly threaded, and helically threaded nails of the same shank diameter using a pneumatic gun in three wood species, for two fabrication conditions at two intervals. Table 18 shows the ratio of threaded to smooth nail end-grain withdrawal capacity for all conditions. In all but four cases, the values indicate that the end-grain withdrawal strength of threaded nails was at least 17% greater than that of smooth shank nails of a similar diameter.

Coated and etched surfaces for nails seem to positively influence immediate end-grain withdrawal performance but, for design, a coated or etched nail should be assumed to behave like a smooth nail. In contrast, the ratio of withdrawal performance of threaded or twisted nails to that of smooth shank nails is unknown, and more research is needed to further classify the influence of thread geometry on end-grain withdrawal. One study indicated a negative influence whereas three other studies indicated a positive influence. In general, nails with surface characteristics appear to have limited advantage over plain nails as far as end-grain withdrawal strength is concerned.

Table 18—Effect of threaded nails on end-grain withdrawal capacity (Lhuede 1985)

Fabrication condition	Time	Wood species	Ratio of threaded to smooth nail withdrawal strength	
			Annularly threaded	Helically threaded
Dry	Immediate	Jarrah	1.29	1.17
		Mountain-ash	1.32	1.03
		Radiata pine	1.20	1.00
	3 months	Jarrah	1.30	1.20
		Mountain-ash	0.97	0.88
Green	Immediate	Jarrah	1.18	1.32
		Messmate	1.24	1.42
	3 months	Jarrah	2.32	2.92
		Messmate	1.45	1.62

Impact Withdrawal

Previous sections in this report have focused on tests in which nails were withdrawn from the wood slowly and at a constant rate. In service, structures can have an impact loading that may give different results than does static loading. Langlands (1933), Borkenhagen and Heyer (1950), and Stern (1970) determined the impact energy required to withdraw a nail from the end and side grain of wood. Because these researchers used different testing procedures, their data sets will be examined individually. Langlands (1933) and Borkenhagen and Heyer (1950) utilized a machine that removed the nail in one blow, whereas Stern (1970) dropped a constant weight from successive heights until the nail withdrew.

Langlands (1933) determined the impact withdrawal energy from the side and end grain for eight different nail surface conditions in western hemlock using a pendulum tester. Immediate impact withdrawal capacity was similar for all nail types, except twisted nails. The effect of nail type was more significant for delayed impact withdrawal capacity. Nails with smooth, cement-coated, and sand-rumbled surfaces had the lowest withdrawal capacity, whereas barbed, twisted, and rusted nails had the highest capacity; the capacity of nails with other surface conditions fell within these extremes. In general, end- to side-grain impact withdrawal ratios were similar for immediate and delayed withdrawal. Because similar ratios were obtained for static and impact side- to end-grain withdrawal, delayed impact withdrawal capacity can be effectively determined from static tests.

Borkenhagen and Heyer (1950) studied the impact withdrawal energy of seven types of nails driven into both the end and side grain and subjected to six moisture change protocols. Figure 14 shows results for box, zinc-coated,

annularly threaded, and helically threaded nails. The trends observed for these four nail types are similar to trends seen for the other three types of nails in this study; similar graphs could be generated for the other nail types from the information given in Table 10.

Figure 14 plots average end-grain impact withdrawal energy against the number of moisture cycles for box, zinc-coated, annularly threaded, and helically threaded nails in eastern white pine and southern yellow pine. All cycles ended with a nail impact withdrawal test from dry wood.

The impact withdrawal energy of both the bright box and zinc-coated nails showed a definite downward trend for the first moisture half-cycle but remained at a near constant level for the remaining cycles. The drop in impact energy in the first half-cycle was more severe in Southern Pine than eastern white pine. For the threaded nails, a general upward trend in impact withdrawal energy occurred with repeated moisture cycles. For the annularly threaded nails in southern yellow pine, this increase occurred only after the first half-cycle (Fig. 14c). Comparison of static (Fig. 9) and impact (Fig. 14) withdrawal results reveals the same general trends for each nail type and species.

Since most of this discussion has focused on the change in end- to side-grain withdrawal ratio, Table 10 includes the end- to side-grain impact withdrawal energy ratio. Borkenhagen and Heyer (1950) found that in southern yellow pine, end- to side-grain impact withdrawal energy ratios ranged from 0.38 to 0.84. In eastern white pine, ratios ranged from 0.39 to 1.01. Figure 15 plots average end- to side-grain static withdrawal ratio against the number of moisture cycles. Both smooth and zinc-coated nails showed a gradual rise in this ratio with an increase in the number of moisture cycles, whereas the response of the threaded nails was nearly constant. In addition, the impact withdrawal ratios for both the smooth and zinc-coated nails were less variable than the static withdrawal ratios. In general, the impact withdrawal ratios were in the same range as the static withdrawal values, except for the zinc-coated nails. These nails had much higher ratios with more variability in the static tests.

Most end- to side-grain impact withdrawal ratios remained constant or slightly increased after moisture cycles compared to immediate impact withdrawal ratios. Therefore, the results indicate that with moisture content cycles, end-grain impact withdrawal energy changes at a rate similar to that of side-grain impact withdrawal energy, so the end- to side-grain ratios are constant.

In Stern's (1970) impact energy research, nails were driven into green wood and either tested immediately or after a 6-week delay (Table 13). For common and box nails, the immediate end- to side-grain impact withdrawal energy ratios were 0.49 and 0.44, respectively, in Southern Pine and 0.63 and 0.51, respectively, in Red Oak. These ratios are

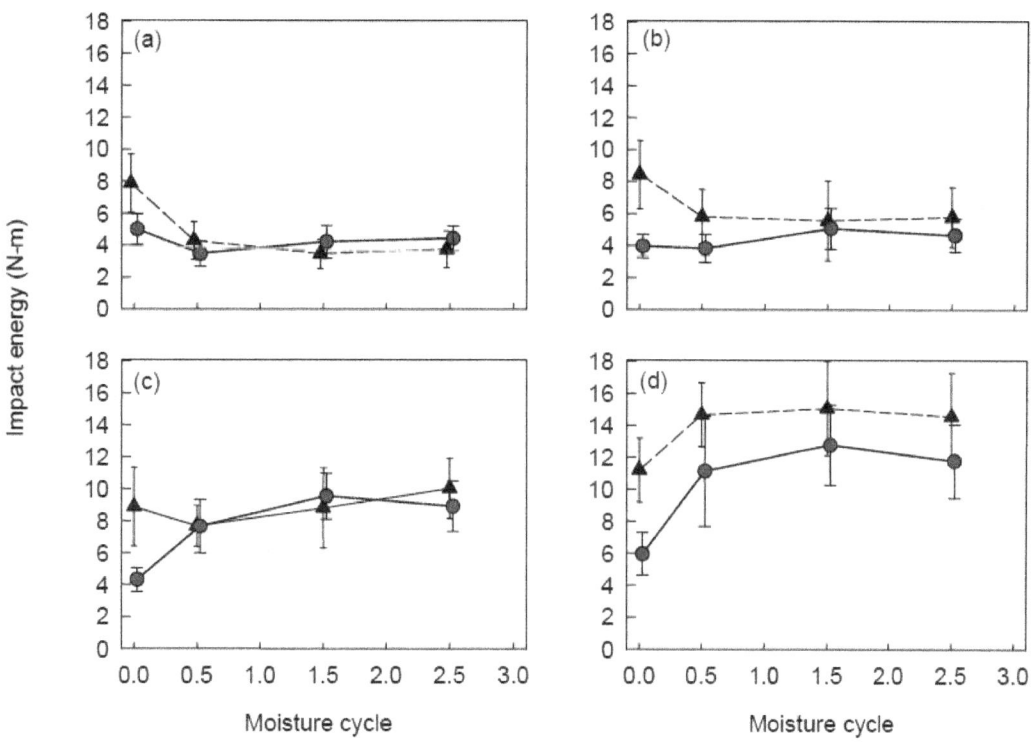

Figure 14—Effect of moisture cycles on impact end-grain withdrawal energy for different nail types in eastern white pine (circles) and southern yellow pine (triangles): (a) box, (b) zinc-coated, (c) annularly threaded, and (d) helically threaded. (Borkenhagen and Heyer 1950)

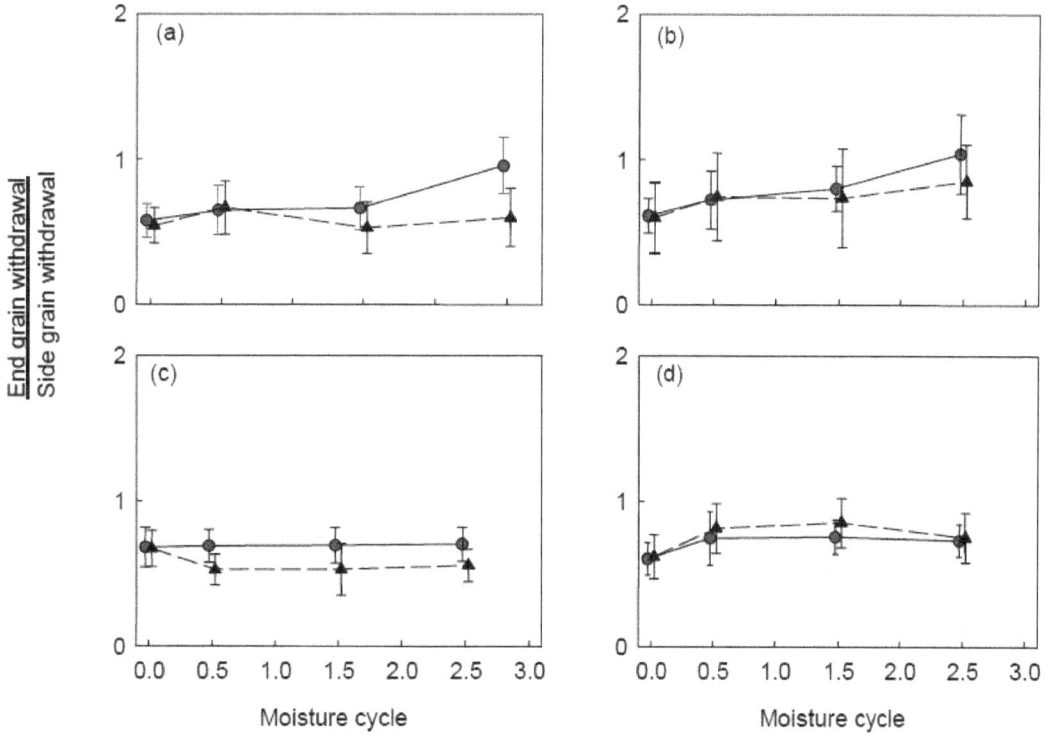

Figure 15—Effect of moisture cycles on impact end- to side-grain withdrawal energy ratio for different nail types in eastern white pine (circles) and southern yellow pine (triangles): (a) box, (b) zinc-coated, (c) annularly threaded, and (d) helically threaded. (Borkenhagen and Heyer 1950)

similar to values found in the static and impact work of Borkenhagan and Heyer. When specimens were allowed to dry for 6 weeks, ratios for three of the four specimens increased significantly. Stern's work suggests an upward trend in the end- to side-grain withdrawal strength ratio, which indicates that end-grain withdrawal energy decreases over time but at a slower rate than does side-grain withdrawal energy.

In all these studies, the end- to side-grain impact withdrawal energy ratios are similar for both immediate withdrawal and withdrawal after moisture cycling. Furthermore, impact and static end- to side-grain ratios are within similar ranges and follow the same trends with change in moisture content. Therefore, the end- to side-grain ratio of static withdrawal tests could be used to estimate end-grain impact withdrawal strength.

End-Nailed Joints

Only a portion of the Scholten and Molander (1950) investigation into joint behavior has been included in this paper. The axial tension load–slip characteristics for end-nailed, toe-nailed, and metal-strapped joints are shown in Figure 4. The joint capacity for all fabricated joints generally increased with the diameter of nail used to fabricate the joint and with the utilization of metal strapping. The maximum slip was smallest for the end-nailed joints and greatest for the metal-strapped joints.

Equation (6) was used to investigate if the change in joint capacity can be predicted. Table 19 shows values for nail geometry, joint specific gravity, and experimental joint withdrawal strength. It also shows the predicted withdrawal capacity of joints calculated by Equation (6). For joints constructed with 3.8-mm- (0.149-in.-) and 4.1-mm- (0.161-in.-) diameter nails, the predicted and experimental loads are within 6%, but for the 4.9-mm- (0.192-in.-) diameter nail, the predicted value is 44% greater than the experimental value. This further indicates that Equation (4), which was developed primarily from data on 2.52-mm- (0.099-in.-) diameter nails, might not valid for predicting the end-grain withdrawal capacity of nails with diameters greater than 4.1 mm (0.161 in.).

Whitney (1977) conducted delayed end-grain joint withdrawal tests for two-nail joints in radiata pine and one- and two-nail joints in Corsican pine. To further investigate if end-grain withdrawal joint capacity can be predicted from Equation (6), experimental and predicted capacities were compared. Predicted values were calculated using the specific gravity values listed in Table 17. Immediate capacity predictions from Equation (6) need to be adjusted to values for delayed capacity predictions. For delayed withdrawal tests of joints fabricated dry and maintained dry, Equation (6) immediate capacity values were reduced by 10%. This reduction represents the decrease in withdrawal capacity observed in Lhuede's radiata pine specimens after a 6-month delay with a change in moisture content. For the delayed withdrawal tests of joints fabricated green and allowed to dry, Equation (6) immediate capacity values were reduced by 43%. This reduction represents the decrease observed in Lhuede's Messmate specimens fabricated green and allowed to condition for 6 months before testing. These results were used to determine the adjustment since the specific gravity of Messmate is similar to that of Corsican and radiata pine. Comparison of the predicted and experimental capacity values indicates that five of the six predictions were conservative. The single over-prediction, for the dry Corsican pine joint containing two nails, was approximately 10% higher than mean test values.

Based on comparisons to the joint withdrawal capacity values found by Scholten and Molander (1950) and Whitney (1977), Equation (6), with appropriate adjustments for conditions of use, apparently yields adequate predictions of actual end-grain joint capacity for nails less than 4.5 mm (0.177 in.) in diameter.

Conclusions

The literature indicates that the statements in the *Wood Handbook* pertaining to nail withdrawal resistance from the end grain of wood are based on the unpublished work of Gahagan and Scholten (1938) and Borkenhagen and Heyer (1950). These statements appear to be founded on significant amounts of experimental data contained in these two reports.

Table 19—Effectiveness of specific gravity relationship for predicting strength of end-nailed joints

Nail size	Nail diameter (mm)	Nail length (mm)	Depth of penetration (mm)	Joint specific gravity	Predicted withdrawal strength (N)	Actual withdrawal strength (N)	Error (%)
10d	3.8	76.2	34.9	0.39	1,090	1,027	6
16d	4.1	88.9	46.6	0.38	1,519	1,432	6
20d	4.9	101.6	60.3	0.41	2,642	1,833	44

Using the data from five independent studies, the relationship between specific gravity and withdrawal strength was derived for smooth shank nails immediately withdrawn from dry wood. The data indicate that the specific gravity–end-grain withdrawal strength expression predicts loads to the same level of accuracy as does the similar side-grain withdrawal strength expression that is utilized in the current design procedures (ASCE 1996, AF&PA 2001). Equation (6) shows that immediate end-grain withdrawal strength predictions are adequate for joints constructed with nails having a diameter of 4.5 mm (0.177 in.) or less.

In all studies, the immediate end- to side-grain withdrawal strength ratio ranges between 0.5 and 0.8, and this ratio is shown to be independent of specific gravity. Except for annularly threaded nails, the immediate end- to side-grain withdrawal strength ratio is similar for all nail types. For annularly threaded nails, the ratio is significantly lower because of the high side-grain withdrawal strength loads.

One study indicates that for smooth shank nails, the end- to side-grain withdrawal ratio increases with an increase in the time between specimen fabrication and nail withdrawal. In other words, the difference between end- and side-grain withdrawal loads decreases after a delay.

After cycles of wetting and drying, end-grain withdrawal values are constant or tend to increase slightly for threaded fasteners, but the withdrawal strength of box and surface-coated nails does not show any clear trend. Threaded fasteners tend to maintain their immediate end- to side-grain withdrawal strength ratio, even after several cycles of wetting and drying, and have much lower variances than do bright box or surface-coated nails. Smooth shank nails, independent of coating type, tend to have end- to side-grain ratios that are constant or increase with moisture cycles and time; that is, the difference between end- and side-grain withdrawal capacity decreases if the ratio increases.

The effect of nail threads on end-grain nail withdrawal strength is unclear. Stern (1950) and Lhuede (1985) report that the withdrawal strength of annularly and helically threaded nails is greater to that of smooth shank nails. However, the data from Borkenhagen and Heyer (1950) shows that threaded nails are less effective than smooth shank nails.

Finally, the ratio of end- to side-grain impact withdrawal energy is similar to that of end- to side-grain static withdrawal strength for both immediate withdrawal and withdrawal after moisture cycling. Therefore, end- to side-grain ratios from static delayed or moisture cycle withdrawal tests could be used to estimate the long-term end-grain impact withdrawal strength from immediate impact energy withdrawal tests.

Recommendations

Nails driven into the end grain of wood do resist both static and impact loads. However, additional research is required in several areas. Of the 4,723 data points on the relationship of specific gravity to nail withdrawal strength, only 294 data points were from tests of nails with a diameter larger than 2.52 mm (0.099 in.). Therefore, research is needed on end-grain withdrawal capacity of nails with a diameter greater than 4.1 mm (0.163 mm) so that Equation (5) can be further developed.

Furthermore, none of the studies evaluated repetitive loading of nails from the end grain since joints in service typically do not experience strictly static or impact loading. Repetitive loading may cause end-grain withdrawal capacity to significantly decrease over time.

There is conflicting data on how threaded nails perform in comparison with smooth shank nails when withdrawn from the end grain. Three studies showed an increase in nail withdrawal capacity whereas one study showed a decrease. Since the use of threaded fasteners in construction is increasing, more research is needed to determine the effects of surface characteristics on end-grain withdrawal.

Finally, more research is needed to determine the long-term withdrawal strength of nails driven into end and side grain. The data in this report suggest that over time end-grain and side-grain withdrawal capacity may become equivalent. Very few test replicates measuring the effect of time delay on withdrawal strength were conducted, and more tests need to be run to clarify these limited observations.

Literature Cited

AF&PA. 2001. National design specification for wood construction. Washington, DC: American Forest & Paper Association.

ASCE. 1996. Load and resistance factored design for engineered wood construction. Reston, VA: American Society of Civil Engineers.

ASTM. 2003. Standard test methods for mechanical fasteners in wood. ASTM D 1761–88. West Conshohocken, PA: American Society for Testing and Materials.

Borkenhagen, E.H.; Heyer, O.C. 1950. Resistance to direct withdrawal of various types of nails driven into green and dry wood and subjected to cycles of wetting and drying. Unpub. Res. Rep. Madison, WI: U.S. Department of Agriculture, Forest Service, Forest Products Laboratory. 23 p.

Forest Products Laboratory. 1999. The wood handbook: wood as an engineering material. Gen. Tech. Rep. FPL–GTR–113. Madison, WI: U.S. Department of Agriculture Forest Service, Forest Products Laboratory. 463 p.

Gahagan, J.M.; Scholten, J.A. 1938. Resistance of wood to the withdrawal of nails. Unpub. Rep. Madison, WI: U.S. Department of Agriculture, Forest Service, Forest Products Laboratory. 58 p.

Huston, H.H. 1947. Direct withdrawal tests of plain, cement-coated, and F.D. coated seven penny box nails. Unpub. Rep. Madison, WI: U.S. Department of Agriculture, Forest Service, Forest Products Laboratory. 6 p.

Langlands, I. 1933. The holding power of special nails. Tech. Pap. 11. Council for Scientific and Industrial Research, Division of Forest Products. 30 p.

Lhuede, E.P. 1985. Side and end grain withdrawal loads for single nails in Australian timber species. CSIRO–Division of Building Research. 12 p.

McLain, T.E. 1997. Design axial withdrawal strength from wood: II. Plain-shank common wire nails. Forest Products Journal. 47(6): 103–109.

Rammer, D.R.; Winistorfer, S.G.; Bender, D.A.; Pollock, D. 2001. Withdrawal strength of threaded nails. ASCE Journal of Structural Engineering. 127(4): 442–449.

Scholten, J.A.; Molander, E.G. 1950. Strength of nailed joints in frame walls. Agricultural Engineering. 31(11): 551–555.

Stern, E.G. 1950. Nails in end-grain lumber. Timber News and Machine Woodworker. 58(2138): 490–492.

Stern, E.G. 1965. Pallets assembled with 10-gauge automatic nails. Forest Products Journal. 15(6): 242–246.

Stern, E.G. 1970. Effectiveness of Senco nails. Virginia Polytechnic Institute Research Division, Wood Research and Wood Construction Laboratory. No. 91. p 43.

Whitney, R.S. 1977. Two-nail versus single nail joints of New Zealand-grown pine. FPRS Proceedings P–77–19. Madison, WI: Forest Products Research Society.

www.ingramcontent.com/pod-product-compliance
Lightning Source LLC
Chambersburg PA
CBHW080754290526
45790CB00008B/3444